OTHER BOOKS BY RANDY ALCORN

NONFICTION
50 Days of Heaven
90 Days of God's Goodness
Does the Birth Control Pill Cause Abortions?
Eternal Perspectives
The Goodness of God
The Grace and Truth Paradox
Heaven
Heaven for Kids
Help for Women Under Stress
If God Is Good
In Light of Eternity
The Law of Rewards
Life Promises for Eternity
Managing God's Money
Money, Possessions and Eternity
ProLife Answers to ProChoice Arguments
The Promise of Heaven
The Purity Principle
The Resolution for Men
Seeing the Unseen
Sexual Temptation: Establishing Guardrails
The Treasure Principle
Touchpoints: Heaven
We Shall See God
Why ProLife?

FICTION
The Chasm
Courageous
Deadline
Deception
Dominion
Edge of Eternity
Eternity
The Ishbane Conspiracy
Lord Foulgrin's Letters
Safely Home
Tell Me About Heaven
Wait Until Then

RANDY ALCORN

hand in HAND

The Beauty of God's Sovereignty and Meaningful Human Choice

MULTNOMAH
BOOKS

HAND IN HAND
PUBLISHED BY MULTNOMAH BOOKS
12265 Oracle Boulevard, Suite 200
Colorado Springs, Colorado 80921

To

Julia Stager
*Not only for your fine work producing the
charts and diagrams I envisioned,
but for your theological insights and
contributions which I so value.*

Gerry Breshears
*For your honest and thoughtful critique
not only of this manuscript but others,
from which I have greatly benefited,
especially when we disagree.*

Doreen Button
*For your above and beyond work as my on-staff editor,
and the countless hours you spend helping
make my books better.*

Ron Norquist
*For giving me the idea to write this book.
Thanks for your life, my old and dear friend!*

*Thanks also to my wife, Nanci, and our dear friends Steve
and Sue Keels for fruitful theological discussions; to Ken
Petersen for believing in the book; to Steve Halliday and
Thomas Womack for fine editing; to Stephanie Anderson and
Bonnie Hiestand for carefully working over the manuscript at
various stages; to Pam Shoup for her extraordinary manage-
ment of the manuscript and Holly Briscoe for her outstanding
fact-checking and copyediting; to Tim Challies and Andy
Naselli for helpful input on the charts and diagrams; and to
the staff and board of Eternal Perspective Ministries who offer
incredible support and friendship. I am deeply grateful to all
who helped, including those I'll remember later that I should
have included! Soli Deo Gloria—to God alone be glory.*

Contents

Why Is This Tough and Controversial Issue Worth Discussing?

Let those who are wise understand these things.
    Let those with discernment listen carefully.
The paths of the LORD are true and right,
    and righteous people live by walking in them.
    But in those paths sinners stumble and fall.

Hosea 14:9, NLT

Let us arouse ourselves to the sternest fidelity, laboring to win souls as much as if it all depended wholly upon ourselves, while we fall back in faith upon the glorious fact that everything rests with the eternal God.

Charles Spurgeon

What difference does it make?

What good can come from studying the mysterious and sometimes upsetting subject of God's sovereignty and human free will?

In small-group Bible studies, at colleges and seminaries, on blogs and radio programs, sovereignty and free will are bantered about. Some recognize these issues as hugely important. Convinced of their position, they look for opportunities to make their case.

Others shrug and say, "These doctrines cause division and are impossible to understand. Why even try?"

I believe one compelling reason to study them is to *better* understand what we cannot *fully* understand. And in the case of God's sovereignty and human choice, while it's not imperative that I understand everything, it *is* important that I believe in both. If I don't believe in God's sovereignty, I'll either despair or imagine that I must carve out my own path. If I don't believe in my freedom to make meaningful choices, I'll either give up on life or not take responsibility for my decisions.

Following are six other excellent reasons:

1. To develop a deeper appreciation for God and his Word, which reveals him to us.

When the United States announced its intention to send a man to the moon, it mobilized untold resources. By the time Neil Armstrong set foot on the lunar surface in July 1969, the US space program had done much more than reach its objective. Along the way, great advances were made in medicine, engineering, chemistry, physics, and numerous other fields. NASA aimed at the moon and got a whole lot more.

Likewise, our pursuit of godly wisdom and understanding will not only deepen our perspective on a specific passage or topic, but also help us in countless other ways, as we give extra effort to diligently and prayerfully meditate on God's Word (see Psalms 19:8; 119:30, 105; 2 Peter 1:19). By the time you finish this book, I hope you'll have learned about God's sovereignty and our choices and a lot more too.

2. To help us mirror Christ's humility.

True humility and wisdom consist of recognizing how little we really know. The Bible insists we "know in part" and we "see but a poor reflection as in a mirror" (1 Corinthians 13:9, 12).

However, God is honored when we go to his Word to learn more about him and his ways. We're to bow to the wisdom of Scripture, even when its mysteries are hard to wrap our minds around. Humility requires that we not think more highly of ourselves than we ought (see Romans 12:3) and that we realize how much we have to learn from God.

When the Ethiopian eunuch was puzzling over Scripture, Philip asked, "Do you understand what you are reading?" (Acts 8:30). Asking God to enlighten us and give us insight from his Word will go a long way toward benefiting from this study.

> True humility and wisdom consist of recognizing how little we really know.

Bible study is exciting when we come expecting to learn, to be challenged, and to be transformed. If you aren't open to adjusting your opinions when they don't align with Scripture, this book is not for you.

3. To embrace all of God's inspired Word, not just parts of it.

"The first to present his case seems right," says Proverbs 18:17, "till another comes forward and questions him." Our families and churches and the books we've read may have presented their cases first, but that doesn't mean they are right.

The Message paraphrases Ecclesiastes 7:18: "It's best to stay in touch with both sides of an issue. A person who fears God deals responsibly with all of reality, not just a piece of it." God inspired *all* of his Word, not just parts of it, and he calls us to embrace it all. My desire in this book is to mine from God's Word "all of reality, not just a piece of it."

We should compare Scripture with Scripture to discern the whole counsel of God.

Large dogs can get two tennis balls in their mouths at the same time. Not our Dalmatian, Moses. He managed to get two in his mouth only momentarily. To his distress, one ball or the other always spurted out. Likewise, we have a hard time handling parallel ideas such as grace *and* truth, or God's sovereignty *and* free or meaningful choice. We need to stretch our undersized minds to hold them both at once.

A paradox is an apparent contradiction, not an actual one. Sovereignty and meaningful choice aren't contradictory. God has no trouble understanding how they work together. In his infinite mind they coexist in perfect harmony.

As you may have noticed, however, *our* minds are not infinite. And while our brains can never fully grasp sovereignty and meaningful choice, by affirming what Scripture says about both, we can avoid the mistake of denying one in order to affirm the other.

> A paradox is an apparent contradiction, not an actual one.

4. To foster unity in the body of Christ.
I bring to this book a respect for brothers and sisters in Christ who believe God's Word but understand it differently than I do. I encourage you to carefully examine your own positions and inconsistencies before subjecting fellow Christians to blistering critique. Puritan Thomas Brooks stated, "There are no souls in the world that are so fearful to judge others as those that do most judge themselves, nor so careful to make a righteous judgment of men or things as those that are most careful to judge themselves."[1]

Let's bear the fruit of the Spirit, which includes both peace and patience (see Galatians 5:22). Unity has an evangelistic power that needless division undermines (see John 17:20–21). When we seek to become peacemakers among Christ-following Bible believers, we please Jesus (see Matthew 5:9).

Let's recognize our core areas of agreement, making an honest attempt to *understand* one another while refusing to let peripheral issues separate us. If we love the same Jesus and believe the same Bible, let's start and end there.

5. To avoid both fatalism and crushing guilt.

Church history shows us that leaning heavily toward a particular set of verses can result in apathy and passivity: "God is going to do whatever he wants to do anyway, so why bother doing anything ourselves?" Leaning heavily toward another set of verses can result in something close to frenzy and unrelenting guilt: "We have to save the world! It all depends on us!"

What is God's role and what is mine? Is my life in God's hands, my hands, or the hands of demons or other people? What we believe about God's sovereignty and human choice has a significant impact on how we live.

6. To prevent us from becoming trivial people in a shallow age.

The times we live in are in no danger of going down in history as "The Era of Deep Thought." In our world, feelings overshadow thinking, and sizzle triumphs over substance.

Taking their cues from the culture, Christians who hear about the paradox of sovereignty and free will might say, "It's a mystery; we're never going to solve it." But this can just be laziness, a spiritual-sounding way of saying, "I don't want to think too hard. Let's watch a movie instead."

How can we keep the shallowness of our culture from turning us into trivial Christians? "Reflect on what I am saying," Paul wrote, "for the Lord will give you insight into all this" (2 Timothy 2:7).

Though surrounded with sweeping superficiality and slavery to what's trending on Twitter, we must learn to think deeply. Paul warned, "The time will come when people will not put up with sound doctrine. Instead, to suit their own desires, they will gather around them a great number of teachers to say what their itching ears want to hear. They will turn their ears away from the truth and turn aside to myths" (2 Timothy 4:3–4, NIV 2011).

If you want truth and depth, you have to spend time in God's Word, allowing it to make the crucial sixteen-inch journey from your head to your heart. Yes, the question of how human choice and divine sovereignty can coexist is big and difficult, but it's also vitally important. If we devote our lives to dealing only with trivial issues, we can't help but become trivial people.

The relationship of God's sovereignty and our meaningful choice is both intriguing and beautiful.

Of all the dilemmas we confront in life, none is more befuddling than God's sovereignty and human choice. So why do I find the perplexing question of God's sovereignty and human choice beautiful rather than frustrating?

It all depends on perspective.

> You don't have to be able to wrap your mind around something in order to see its beauty.

When astronomers gaze into deep space they're confronted with the universe's puzzles. One of them is dark energy, which is "thought to be the enigmatic force that is pulling the cosmos apart at ever-increasing speeds." How and why is it doing this? Another unknown is how dark matter, "thought to make up about 23 percent of the universe," somehow has "mass but cannot be seen"; its existence is deduced by the "gravitational pull it exerts on regular matter." What exactly is it?

Cosmic rays are highly energetic particles that flow into our solar system from deep in outer space, but where do they actually come from? It's been a mystery for fifty years. The sun's corona, its ultrahot outer atmosphere, has a temperature of "a staggering 10.8 million degrees Fahrenheit." Solar physicists still don't understand how the sun reheats itself.[2]

These mysteries and countless others have not so much frustrated scientists as fascinated them. Watch their interviews and read their articles; their wonder about things they don't comprehend is palpable. You don't have to be able to wrap your mind around something in order to see its beauty.

This is how I view the conundrum of God remaining sovereign while still granting his creatures the gift of choice. The immensity of the marvel itself should move God's children to worship.

Human beings are capable of inventing nonliving machines, including computers they program to do complex tasks. But God goes far beyond that by creating complex beings with choice-making capacity, including the freedom to worship or revolt.

For God to fully know in advance what billions of human beings could and would do under certain circumstances, and to govern our world in such a way as to accomplish his eternal plan—is this not stunning?

If we can gaze at the night sky or a waterfall or the ocean with hearts moved at their sheer beauty, should we not be able to study the metaphysical wonders of God's universe with equal or even greater awe?

Surely our lives are greatly enriched when we recognize the mysterious beauty of the interplay between God's ways and ours.

God's choices come first, and ours second.

Throughout this book, I'll discuss both choice and sovereignty in ways that may frustrate you if you're accustomed to affirming one at the expense of the other. I may irritate you by sometimes making what I believe seem obvious, and at other times raising questions that challenge all positions, including my own. To try to tie everything together neatly wouldn't do justice to the complexity of these difficult issues.

I do think it's reasonable to look at God's choices as being more foundational than our own. Why? Because we're made in his image, and his choice-making precedes and empowers ours. The universe is first and foremost about the purposes, plan, and glory of God. Because he is infinite, his choices naturally hold more sway than those of his creatures. As his power exceeds ours, so does the power of his choices.

That doesn't mean our choices don't matter—they certainly do. He gives us room to make choices according to the prevailing disposition of our will and within the limits he imposes in his sovereign plan. My perspective is simply that everything about God, including his choices, is greater than everything about us.

A. W. Tozer said, "Every soul belongs to God and exists by His pleasure. God being Who and What He is, and we being who and what we are, the only thinkable relation between us is one of full lordship on His part and complete submission on ours."[3]

That's the spirit in which I'm approaching this book: eager to acknowledge his lordship and willing to submit to whatever he has revealed in his Word. I invite you to join me in exploring this fascinating topic... and experiencing the joy of discovery.

Notes

The opening epigraph is from C. H. Spurgeon, in George Carter Needham, *The Life and Labors of Charles H. Spurgeon* (Boston: D. L. Guernsey, 1883), 12.

1. Thomas Brooks, *Precious Remedies Against Satan's Devices* (CreateSpace Independent Publishing Platform, 2010), 154.

2. Space.com Staff, "8 Baffling Astronomy Mysteries," April 3, 2013, numbers 8, 7, and 1, www.space.com/15936-astronomy-mysteries -science-countdown.html.

3. A. W. Tozer, *The Pursuit of God* (Rockville, MD: Serenity, 2009), 89.

2

An Invitation to Calvinists, Arminians, and Those Who Don't Know the Difference

All that the Father gives me will come to me, and whoever comes to me I will never cast out.

John 6:37, ESV

The Spirit and the Bride say, "Come."… Let the one who is thirsty come; let the one who desires take the water of life without price.

Revelation 22:17, ESV

How many Calvinists does it take to change a light bulb? *None. Only God can change a light bulb. Since he has ordained the darkness and predestined when the lights will come on, stay seated and trust him.*

How many Arminians does it take to change a light bulb? *Only one. But first the bulb must want to be changed.*

What does a Calvinist say after he falls down three flights of stairs? *"Glad to get that out of the way."*

How do you confuse a Calvinist?

Take him to a buffet and tell him he can choose whatever he wants.
Calvinists have their TULIP;[1] what flower do Arminians prefer?
*The daisy. Why? "He loves me, he loves me not. He loves me, he loves
me not..."*

Okay, be honest: which jokes made you laugh? I hope you see some
humor in your own position. And if you don't know what Calvinism and
Arminianism are—well, hopefully this chapter will help.

Scripture is always inspired, but sometimes annoying.
I once spoke to eighty college students about a sensitive theological question: "Can true Christians lose their salvation?" First, I asked them to
commit themselves to a yes or no answer. I separated them, according to
their answers, on opposite sides of the room, breaking them up into small
groups.

Next I gave everyone a handout featuring twenty passages of Scripture. After reading these aloud, the students were to discuss in their groups
and decide: "If these were the only Scripture passages I had, would I answer the question yes or no?"

Tensions rose. On both sides of the room, students looked confused,
and some were angry.

Only afterward did I explain that I'd given each group *different* hand-
outs consisting of entirely different passages. The Scriptures each group
was given appeared to teach an answer exactly *opposite* to the position
they'd said they believed.

My main take-away was that we need to establish our positions in
light of *all* Scripture, not just our preferred passages that support what we
wish to believe.

The issue of whether Christians can lose their salvation is one that
involves matters of God's sovereignty and human choice. The question
typically gets one answer from those called Arminians and the opposite
answer from those called Calvinists. John Wesley is seen as the classic
Arminian, while John Calvin (surprise!) is the classic Calvinist; but, trust
me, neither Calvin nor Wesley were idiots (which I wanted to help those
eighty college students understand).

Unfortunately, the terms *Calvinist* and *Arminian,* while generally helpful, suggest many inaccurate assumptions and stereotypes. Some Calvinists are radically different from others, and the same can be said for Arminians. As general descriptions of theology, Calvinism and Arminianism can be helpful terms, but they're decidedly unhelpful when it leads to the kind of thinking (for either group) that concludes, "They all believe A, and none of them believes B."

> The Bible features a staggering breadth and depth of truth that selective proof-texting can never reflect.

Modern Calvinists often emphasize certain aspects of Calvin's writings and doctrine more than others. They may overlook, for example, Calvin's emphasis on our mystical union with Christ and the Holy Spirit, or miss the warmth of Calvin's love for Christ. They may never have read how Calvin detested those "who are content to roll the gospel on the tips of their tongues when its efficacy ought to penetrate the inmost affections of the heart, take its seat in the soul, and affect the whole man a hundred times more deeply than the cold exhortations of the philosophers!"[2]

Similarly, modern Arminians are often less Calvinistic than Arminius was. For instance, some speak disparagingly of the doctrine of total depravity which Arminius affirmed, as did Wesley. On the other hand, many of them reject the Wesleyan doctrine of sinless perfectionism, which Arminius did not hold to.

Both "sides" love God and believe his Word, but they emphasize different portions of it. Therefore the common attitude, "If you really believed the Bible, you would agree with me," reflects a far too simplistic approach.

If we want to better understand any doctrine or teaching, we must consider not bits and pieces of the Bible but "the whole counsel of God" (Acts 20:27, ESV). The Bible features a staggering breadth and depth of truth that selective proof-texting can never reflect.

We need to look from both sides of the fence.
In this book, we're tackling two truths that seem to contradict each other. The temptation will be to major on one, then negate or minimize the other. The alternative is to embrace both.

Charles Spurgeon's answer was to recognize that whatever God's Word teaches is true, whether or not it all makes sense to us. He said,

> I see in one place, God presiding over all in providence; and yet I see, and I cannot help seeing, that man acts as he pleases, and that God has left his actions to his own will, in a great measure.... If, then, I find taught in one place that everything is fore-ordained, that is true; and if I find in another place that man is responsible for all his actions, that is true; and it is my folly that leads me to imagine that two truths can ever contradict each other. These two truths, I do not believe, can ever be welded into one upon any human anvil, but one they shall be in eternity: they are two lines that are so nearly parallel, that the mind that shall pursue them farthest, will never discover that they converge; but they do converge, and they will meet somewhere in eternity, close to the throne of God, whence all truth doth spring.[3]

Historically, Calvinism and Arminianism have each held to a belief in both God's sovereignty and meaningful human choice. But they've held those beliefs in different ways. Calvinists have tended to emphasize God's sovereignty, Arminians human choice.

What is Arminianism?
Arminianism is a worldview associated with Dutch theologian Jacob Arminius (1560–1609) and evangelist John Wesley (1703–91). While there are major differences in the shape of their theologies and those developed by their followers, I'll focus on their common perspectives in the areas of sovereignty, free will, and human responsibility.

The American Heritage Dictionary defines *Arminian* as "of or relating to the theology of Jacobus Arminius and his followers, who rejected the Calvinist doctrines of predestination and election and who believed that human free will is compatible with God's sovereignty."[4]

This is accurate. However, many Calvinists call themselves "compatibilists" because they too believe human free will is compatible with God's sovereignty. Yet they see this compatibility in different ways than Arminians do.

A Calvinist wrote, "Arminianism is the rejection of predestination, and a corresponding affirmation of the freedom of the human will."[5] An Arminian might respond, "Actually, I *do* believe predestination is taught in the Bible. However, my *understanding* of predestination is different from yours."

Calvinists have tended to emphasize God's sovereignty, Arminians human choice.

From years sitting under Arminian teaching in the wonderful church where I first trusted Jesus, I understand that particular view of sovereignty and free will. It includes these aspects: God is sovereign, on the throne, and working out a plan—and one day Christ will return and rule the earth. Meanwhile we pray, "Your will be done," realizing God's will is being violated all around us and by us daily. Satan is real and powerful, though of course God is infinitely greater.

All evangelical Arminians recognize that human nature was damaged seriously through the Fall. However, they believe humans still retain the freedom of contrary choice. That is, we don't have to choose one way; we can instead choose another. They believe in voluntary free will. They argue that contrary choice cuts to the depths of our true personhood: "A choice that actually can go but one way is not a choice, and without this 'freedom' there is not personality."[6]

As an Arminian, I was taught that God offers sufficient grace to every sinner to examine the gospel, believe it, and repent of their sins. I was also taught, however, that God doesn't normally interfere with our freedom to choose. Whether a person goes to Heaven or Hell depends on what he, in his free will, chooses. No one could be saved without the work of Jesus, and everyone needs the Spirit's assistance to be saved, but the individual is free to accept or reject Christ. All people receive God's enabling grace, called prevenient grace. They experience a *freed* will, a will capable of accepting as well as rejecting the free gift of salvation in Jesus. Arminians understand Ephesians 2:8–9 like this: "For it is by grace you have been saved, through faith—and this [grace and/or salvation] not from yourselves, it is the gift of God—not by works, so that no one can boast."

Arminius quoted Bernardus to make this key point: "No one, except God, is able to bestow salvation; and nothing, except free will, is capable of receiving it [cf. John 1:12]."[7]

No one can be saved without God's grace, but neither can he be saved without exercising his faith to accept that gift. In this sense, the believer's faith is his gift to God.

Evangelical Arminians do not believe faith is in any sense a work that merits salvation; Calvinists think that if such faith is from the person, coming from the initiative of her own freely willed choice to say yes to prevenient grace, then the person making the choice would deserve some credit for it, and therefore it would be a work earning her salvation.

What is Calvinism?

The American Heritage Dictionary defines *Calvinism* as "the religious doctrines of John Calvin, emphasizing the omnipotence of God and the salvation of the elect by God's grace alone."[8]

Most Calvinists would say it differently but probably grant this is fairly close. Most Arminians would respond, "But I too believe in God's omnipotence and salvation by grace!"

Calvinist Tim Challies writes, "A Calvinist is someone who rejects the Arminian concept of free will, believing that the will of all humans is bound by their sinful nature and will remain bound until God performs His regenerative work."[9]

Calvinists agree with Arminians that people have the ability to choose.

However, they believe that sinners can only act according to the prevailing disposition of their will. Since the Fall, the human will is in bondage to a sin nature. So the choices of a fallen will are confined to the limits of a sin nature. Hence the Calvinist view of free will is more narrow than the Arminian view. Calvinists believe people are the active agents in their choices, are not forced (from the outside) to make those choices, and are fully responsible for their choices. They don't believe people are able to choose contrary to their natures.

Calvinists affirm people are free to choose according to their natures, but that is not as expansive a freedom as it's typically portrayed. Countless elements make up our natures that were not matters of our choices. We didn't choose our genes, gender, physical abilities, mental capacities, parents, siblings, birthplace, upbringing, childhood influences, education, or many of the untold thousands of circumstances that shaped us. All of these factors played a huge role in the people we became and the choices we make. Regardless of all these dynamics, and some good choices we hopefully made along the way, we have sin natures. That is, we are not sinners because we sin; we sin because we are sinners. So yes, people choose to do what they want, but *sinners want to sin.* Therefore the sinner is incapable of choosing to follow God unless God first empowers him. He is dead in his trespasses, no more capable of cooperating to make himself alive than Lazarus could cooperate with Jesus in raising himself from the dead.

Salvation requires a transforming work of grace (regeneration or effectual call). When, by God's grace, people are born again, only then do they experience a will capable of choosing righteousness, which some call a truly *freed* will (a term Arminians associate with prevenient grace, in which God frees people to be able to choose whether or not to believe in Christ).

Calvinists understand Ephesians 2:8–9 like this: "By grace you have been saved, through faith—and this [not just grace or salvation, but *faith*] is not from yourselves, it is the gift of God—not by works, so that no one can boast." Note that evangelical Arminians and Calvinists both believe the Bible. They're equally committed, for instance, to the truth of Ephesians 2:8–9. But they interpret the verses differently when it comes to whether or not our faith in God is his gift to us or our gift to him.

Do Arminians reject God's sovereignty?

One Calvinist wrote, "Arminians teach that God is frustrated by the free will of his creatures."[10] But would any Arminian say it that way? When I was an Arminian, I never would have.

Another Calvinist, in a spirit of fairness, pointed out that most Arminians do believe in God's sovereignty:

> To say that God gives people freedom does not necessarily mean that God relinquishes his authority over mankind. To be sovereign does not mean that one always has to be in meticulous control over everything that happens. God, for the Arminian, could shape all human events according to his will, he just chooses not to. This is still sovereignty.[11]

Arminian theologian Roger Olson expresses a common frustration: "It is apparent to Arminians that distorted information about Arminian theology plagues contemporary Calvinist students, pastors and lay people.... Simply denying that Arminians believe in God's sovereignty...is so blatantly false that it boggles Arminians' minds."[12]

For the first ten years of my Christian life I read mostly Arminian books, by the hundreds. Occasionally I would read a Calvinist book, only to be amazed at what the writer thought people like me believed! When people tell you that you believe what you don't, it raises your defenses and impairs your ability to trust the other things they say.

Arminians do believe in God's sovereignty. They understand it to mean that God isn't accountable to anyone and can do whatever he wishes. His plans and purposes cannot be overcome. God does what he wants, but what he wants is to have creatures who possess the ability to freely do or not do what he wants! Some people mean by sovereignty that whatever happens is God's will, exactly as he wanted it to happen. Others mean that God maintains control of the universe even when he permits his creatures to violate his will.

Do Calvinists reject the human ability to choose?

Now I'm mostly on the other side of the fence. Though I disagree with many statements made by various Calvinists, I am mainly Calvinist and am sometimes startled when an Arminian assumes I believe things that actually are utterly foreign to my thinking.

One Arminian represents Calvinism by saying, "Even though people might *think* they have the choice to repent, they are making a wrong assumption according to the Calvinist. If they *don't* repent, they are actually doing the only thing they can do.... *They are making no choice at all in the matter of salvation.*"[13]

I'd heard this misconception of Calvinism when I was an Arminian. But I hadn't read many Calvinist books before realizing Calvinists do, of course, believe in human choice. As Arminian theologian F. L. Forlines points out, "In both Calvinism and Arminianism, *the individual does make a choice.* There is no such thing as human personality changing from unbelief to faith without making a choice."[14]

So don't listen to people who argue that Arminians don't believe in God's sovereignty and that Calvinists don't believe in human choice. Instead, seek to understand what similar and different things Arminians and Calvinists *mean* by their use of those terms.

In all fairness, if you want to know what either group believes, ask someone who holds to the position. Never count on the objectivity of information about a position offered by those who argue against it! Though I've labored hard to be evenhanded in this book, the truth is, try as we might, we're always most fair to our own position.

The five points of Calvinism and Arminianism reflect the central importance of the issues of sovereignty and free will.

The five points of Calvinism are often depicted through the acronym TULIP, standing for Total depravity, Unconditional election, Limited atonement, Irresistible grace, and the Perseverance of the saints.

The theology behind TULIP goes back to the Reformation. The Reformer Arminius's supporters issued the Five Articles of Remonstrance in 1610, containing five major points summarizing their disagreements with Calvinistic beliefs. Essentially, these were the five points of Arminianism. In reaction to these five articles, leaders of the Calvinist (or Reformed) movement met and codified their own articles of faith, the Canons of Dort, in 1619. These became the five points of Calvinism.

In the five points on the following chart, notice that the issues of God's choice and human choice, God's sovereignty and our free will, permeate each point. If some points don't seem to relate to sovereignty and free will, look again. They do.

	Calvinism	Arminianism
Human Nature and Freedom	1. **Total Depravity.** People are free to follow their desires, but because of their natures are dead in sin; they do not and cannot desire to repent and turn to God. They have a *complete inability* to respond to God and accept his gift of eternal life, apart from his infusion of saving grace. God is the one and only agent in regeneration, who provides not only the offer of justification in Christ but also the ability to believe the gospel.	1. **Total Depravity** was affirmed by both Arminius and Wesley. All are sinners, in need of salvation. God has given each person the *assisted ability*, through divine enablement, to repent and turn to him. This is *only* as enabled by God's prevenient grace in which he allows but does not cause free-will faith in Christ. There are two agents cooperating in conversion, God and people, but only one agent—God's Spirit—in the resulting regeneration.

Choice of Who Will Be Saved	**2. Unconditional Election.** God chose before creation, not based on foreseen faith or human choices, which sinners he will grant faith and repentance. The determinative choice is not man's; eventually, all whom God has chosen, by his empowerment, will desire salvation and respond to the gospel in faith.	**2. Conditional Election.** God chose in advance to save those whom he foresaw would freely place their faith in Christ. God offers salvation to all and enables any to believe who will, but people themselves fully determine whether or not they will accept God's gift and be saved.
Who Christ Died For	**3. Limited atonement.** Christ died only for the elect. He paid the redemptive price for specific chosen people. The gospel should be preached to all, since God uses human means to draw his elect, who are unknown to men. This is also called definite atonement or particular redemption. Some Calvinists (sometimes called four-pointers or "moderate Calvinists") take issue with this point, believing Christ died for the sins of all people.	**3. Christ died for all people.** Christ's death provided full payment for all sins of all humans, and his atonement is enough for every person to be saved, should each individual accept his gift. His offer of blood-bought salvation is for all. But its efficacy is limited to or realized only by *personal faith,* which is a free-will response. Christ's death can save all but is effective only for those who believe and say yes to Christ and the gospel.

	Calvinism	Arminianism
Grace: Saving and Prevenient	**4. Irresistible Grace.** God's saving grace can't be ultimately rejected (though it can be temporarily resisted). He unilaterally regenerates the elect, granting faith and eternal life. Saving grace is effectually applied to those whom he has chosen to save. In God's timing, he overcomes human resistance to the gospel. Salvation is entirely in his hands, not his creatures'.	**4. The gospel of God's grace is an offered invitation, not a coercive demand.** God grants everyone prevenient grace, genuinely drawing, inviting, and enabling each person to believe without guaranteeing anyone will. God's saving grace is fully effective for all who believe (Calvinists agree). God invites all to be saved but never over-rules a person's decision to reject his grace.
Endurance and Eternal Security of God's People	**5. Perseverance of the Saints.** God saves people and guarantees that those he has chosen (though not all who profess) will continue in saving faith and go to Heaven. Believers persevere because God makes sure none will be lost. He wrote their names in the Book of Life; nothing they do can erase them. True believers can and do sin, but do not continue in long-term willful sin. Calvinists prefer "perseverance" to "eternal security."	**5. Believers may forfeit salvation.** It is a freely received gift that can later be freely rejected. One who'd go to Heaven if he died today could reject Christ later, then go to Hell. Through free will, believers had a part in their names appearing in the Book of Life; if they turn away, their names are removed. God never determines our choice in salvation. (Some "four-point" Arminians believe since God alone regenerates, salvation can't be lost.)

Logically, both systems are coherent, which explains why those who believe any of the points of one position often believe the others. But not always.

For instance, as a young Christian I was a four-point Arminian (a one-point Calvinist), my only Calvinistic belief being that a true Christian could not lose his salvation. Though nearly everyone in my church was Arminian in theology, there was close to an even split on whether or not salvation could be lost. I agreed that many passages appeared, on their face, to say salvation could be lost, but to me the clearest and most irrefutable passages (such as John 10:27–28) seemed to state that it can't be.

As years passed and I studied Scripture, my mind gradually changed on three of the other points. (What's true for many others was true also for me: what we believe the Bible teaches can change over time; Calvinists become more Arminian, Arminians more Calvinistic.) While I could see many passages compatible with limited atonement, I couldn't see passages that emphatically taught it. But I did see some that seemed, and still seem, to teach that Christ died for all people, not just the elect (such as Isaiah 53:6; John 1:29; 1 Timothy 2:6, 4:10; Hebrews 2:9; 2 Peter 2:1; 1 John 2:2). Hence, I'm a four-point Calvinist.[15]

This means I've been both an Arminian and a Calvinist, without ever being *entirely* one or the other. I'm what some call a "moderate Calvinist" and others an "inconsistent Calvinist." I was once a moderate or inconsistent Arminian. But whatever the terminology, I've never been 100 percent in either camp.

I say this not to defend four-point Calvinism, but to illustrate that people can and do believe in some parts of a theological system and not others. I'm not at all unique in this. In my experience, there are many Arminians who believe salvation can't be lost and many Calvinists who believe Christ died for all people. Many draw their conclusions on each of the five points not *from* the points (which are man-made in their particular wording) but from their understanding of God-breathed Scripture.

If staying consistent with a system is our priority, we'll wear lenses that allow us to always see Scripture as making inferences we would never see were we not bringing our theology to the text and trying to make the text harmonize with it. Meanwhile we may explain away what appears to be the clear meaning of texts by reinterpreting them to say something counterintuitive to their wording (*elect* doesn't mean elect, *all* does not mean all). Attempting to stay within a particular system of thought is understandable, yet it's dangerous when we read into texts what no one could or would see there unless they were trying to.

On the issue of God's sovereignty relative to human choice and responsibility, we would do well to refuse to read doctrines into texts where they aren't present. This will keep us from undermining God's sovereignty with human choice or dismantling human choice with God's sovereignty. We shouldn't choose between the kinds of passages we'll deal with in chapters 3 and 4. We should believe both truths, whether or not we can harmonize them.

There are three-point Arminians and three-point Calvinists. Many of both persuasions insist we must be 100 percent one and 0 percent the other. Some five-point Calvinists have a name for four-point Calvinists: Arminians.[16] Others say "there are no four-point Calvinists,"[17] though wishing doesn't make it so. Others recognize that there have always been Calvinists who affirm that Christ died for all people.[18] And some point to Calvin's writings where, in a number of places, he appears to affirm unlimited atonement.[19] (Elsewhere he clearly defends the opposite.)

The all-or-nothing positions on Calvinism or Arminianism would be true only if the system of thought, not the Bible, were fully inspired by God and the authority to which we should bow. Our goal, however, should be consistency with what we believe the Bible actually teaches, not what we think should logically follow from particular doctrines.

It's impossible to say precisely what all Calvinists believe or all Arminians believe. There is diversity within both ways of thinking. At best we can say what most of them believe or what many have historically believed. You cannot know what any particular Calvinist or Arminian believes until you ask that person, or until he or she volunteers it. (And sometimes after listening, you *still* won't know, because the person isn't so sure, or attaches different meanings to key words than you do.)

Calvinism's and Arminianism's differing views of God's choices and creature choices permeate many other doctrines too.

The following chart is my attempt to compare Calvinist and Arminian beliefs about sovereignty and free will as well as seven other subjects. There's a little overlap with the earlier five-points chart, but most of this chart's contents are new and different.

It is, depending on how you look at it, either a brave or foolish thing to try to summarize two controversial perspectives on nine volatile issues, especially since on each issue many on "the same side" disagree with each other. And even those who agree might word their beliefs differently. Nonetheless, I've tried to be accurate and fair, getting input from both Calvinist and Arminian theologians.

	Calvinism	Arminianism
Sovereignty	God controls all, including the most undesirable life details; he can influence or overrule human desires and decisions to accomplish his will. As bad as things look, he has a purpose and plan.	God is over all, accountable to no one, does whatever he pleases, but respects free choice; he rules yet doesn't overrule. Much of the present world, its sin and suffering, is not what he desires.
Foreknowledge	God determines who he "knows" in a relational sense, (i.e., who he plans to redeem); he foreknows and chooses them personally. God knows the future because he decrees the future.	Through God's omniscience he knows in advance all that will happen. This is prescience, or "simple foreknowledge," in which God knows all future events, including conversions, but does not typically determine them.

	Calvinism	Arminianism
Election	Unconditional: God chooses whom he will save and draws them to himself.	Conditional: God chooses whom he will save based on his foreknowledge of who will choose to follow him.
Predestination	God has determined from all eternity whatever will come to pass and works his sovereign will in his entire creation, according to his pre-determined plan. By God's eternal decree, he foreordained eternal life for his chosen and damnation for those who reject him.	God has predestined salvation to all who believe in Jesus and damnation for those who don't. But he doesn't predestine anyone to become and remain a believer, or to remain an unbeliever. This is up to the individual's free choice, which God foreknows but does not determine.
Grace	God gives the elect effectual grace, unilaterally regenerating them, then granting them saving faith and eternal life.	God gives everyone pre-venient grace, enabling all to believe without assuring it. He regenerates those who choose to believe.
Faith	God gives faith to sinners; they do not supply it themselves. Moderate Calvinists might call it a choice of the person which is a guaranteed result of God's effectual grace.	The believer accepts God's offer and trusts in God's promise. The believer responds freely to God's gracious invitation.

Salvation	Monergism: God alone works to bring about new birth and faith within his chosen children, so there can be no doubt who gets the credit.	Synergism: God invites and humans respond with faith, resulting in God's unilateral work of new birth.
Security	Since God does the work of saving, he will assure that those saved will persevere; what can't be earned can't be lost.	Since God never overrides human choice in matters of salvation, a believer may choose to turn away and forfeit salvation.
Sin Nature	All are totally depraved, inheriting a sin nature from Adam. We are not only slaves to sin but dead in sin. We lack the ability to choose the grace God offers us; our wills must first be made alive by God.	All are totally depraved, inheriting a sin nature from Adam. We are in bondage to sin and can't exercise good will toward God apart from supernatural grace, but he gives us all the freedom to choose or reject Him.
Free Will	Our free choices are determined by our desires but not coerced by external authorities. The unsaved are dead in sin, their wills in bondage. By God's common grace, they can make some good choices but cannot in themselves choose to believe in Jesus. Only God can produce saving faith in human hearts.	We have contrary choice; no decision is forced; we are always free to choose within the limits of our sin-damaged wills. The unsaved have wills in bondage until God's prevenient grace enables them to believe in him if they so choose, but God never causes them to believe; that is their choice, not his.

The "determinism continuum" in the following diagram depicts Calvinism and Arminianism, and the viewpoints that fall under them. The farther to the left on the continuum, the more the viewpoint believes that God determines whatever happens. The farther to the right on the continuum, the more the viewpoint believes that human choices, demonic choices, and random forces influence the course of world events—though God is sovereign, he does not control human or demonic choices and natural events, but one day he will return and set up his eternal kingdom and establish his reign.

The viewpoint held by most Calvinists is called compatibilism; the one held by most Arminians is called libertarianism. After dealing with the Bible's revelation of God's sovereignty in chapter 3 and meaningful choice in chapter 4, I'll discuss in chapter 5 libertarianism and compatibilism, to help explore more completely Arminianism and Calvinism and the differences between them. I'll also discuss the viewpoint called Molinism, which is in the middle on the chart because its core distinctives can be embraced by either Calvinists or Arminians.

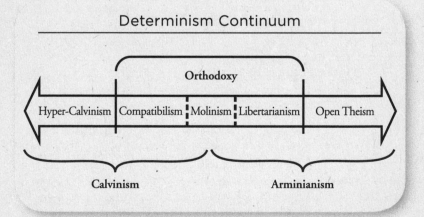

On the far left of the determinism continuum is the extreme of hyper-Calvinism, which holds that God determines every single thought and action of every demon and human being, so that there is no real creature choice at all (more on this in chapter 5). On the far right is the extreme of open theism (see chapter 6), which so emphasizes the power of creaturely free will that it effectively minimizes both God's knowledge and his sovereignty. Both of these extremes, I believe (some will disagree), fall outside of orthodoxy, while mainstream Calvinism and Arminianism fall within it.

Both Calvinists and Arminians can be orthodox, but neither is necessarily orthodox; it depends on their specific beliefs. Arminians who believe they're saved because of their works and Calvinists who believe they're saved by their doctrine, for instance, are certainly not orthodox, and the chart should not be understood to state otherwise.

Orthodoxy involves accepting the essentials of faith as taught by Scripture and historically held by believers. The problem with defining orthodoxy is that different people see different aspects of Christianity as "essential." Some generally accepted essentials, central to orthodoxy, are as follows:

- Jesus Christ, born of a virgin, is fully God and fully man.
- He died for our sins and physically rose from the dead.
- There is only one God, who is triune, holy, and loving.
- The Bible is inspired by God, and entirely authoritative.
- Humans are sinful, separated from their sinless Creator.
- Humans are accountable and will face God's judgment.
- Salvation is through Christ alone.
- Salvation is by grace, through faith, not by human works.
- Believers will be resurrected to eternal life and unbelievers to eternal death.

While this list is neither authoritative nor exhaustive, I think it's something most orthodox Christians would affirm. When I refer to "mainstream" Calvinists and Arminians being "orthodox," I'm speaking of the large number in both camps who confess such orthodox beliefs.

Notice what is *not* on the above list: a precise definition of God's sovereignty, the nature of free will, predestination, or the possibility of losing salvation.

When people hold views that deviate from or twist one or more of Christianity's essential doctrines, those beliefs are heretical. When people disagree on secondary issues of faith (such as the role of women in ministry, whether sign gifts are present today, the nature of the millennium, or the timing of the rapture), those disagreements can be real and passionate, but both parties remain under the umbrella of orthodoxy.

A number of Calvinists believe Arminianism is not orthodox, just as a number of Arminians believe Calvinism is not orthodox. But it's essential to go to Calvinists if you want to know what Calvinists believe and to Arminians if you want to know what Arminians believe. Even the best-intentioned critics often don't get their opponents' views correct.

Going online isn't always a good idea, but there you'll bump into opinions such as these:

- "Calvinism is very much like a rigged carnival game."[20]
- "Arminianism is darkness, wickedness, evil, and heresy of the worst kind."[21]
- "Calvinism is evil."[22]
- "All Arminians are unsaved."[23]

Well...let's just share our honest opinions, shall we?

Some Calvinists insist Arminians think they'll get to Heaven because they were good enough or smart enough to choose Jesus, and hence believe in salvation by works. Some Arminians dismiss Calvinists as believing in a "monster God" who delights in sending people to Hell. They stereotype Calvinists as opposing evangelism and not caring about people. They question whether Calvinists can be saved.

I can assure you that when I was an Arminian, I didn't believe in salvation by works, and that my Arminian church preached salvation by grace through faith and nothing else. I can also assure you that as a Calvinist, I don't follow a monster God, and I love people and believe just as much in evangelism as I did when I was an Arminian.

Let's not condemn people for our interpretation of their terminology or what we've heard they believe. Instead, let's ask them what they really do believe. Calvinists may be surprised to see the depth of what an Arminian believes about the darkness of the human heart and the wonders of God's grace, and Arminians might be surprised to see how the love of

God moves a Calvinist to tears and passionate outreach to the unsaved, weak, and needy.

Why do Calvinists and Arminians misrepresent each other's beliefs?

A Calvinist calls Arminianism "a damnable heresy."[24] An Arminian claims, "Theistic fatalism would be but another name for Calvinist."[25]

A Calvinist argues, "Arminians believe they saved themselves.... Man must save himself by adding his faith.... Man is a co-redeemer with God. And this is works salvation."[26]

You won't hear an Arminian talk like this. To some Calvinists, this *seems* to be the logical conclusion of Arminian doctrine, but that's *not* how the Arminian thinks.

An Arminian wrote, "We're just playthings in God's hands! That's pretty much what 'Reformed' (Calvinistic) Christians believe."[27]

Really? Is that what any Calvinist actually *says* he believes? Or is it the writer's own deduction based on what he supposes Calvinists are saying?

Roger Olson, who rightly bemoans how Calvinists often misrepresent Arminian theology, says this about Calvinism: "God is thereby rendered morally ambiguous at best and a moral monster at worst.... This kind of Calvinism, which attributes everything to God's will and control, makes it difficult (at least for me) to see the difference between God and the devil."[28] Obviously, Olson interprets Calvinism differently than do the Calvinists he critiques.

In fact, most Calvinists have no trouble differentiating between God and the devil! And, despite what some Calvinists have told me, when I was an Arminian I was not a "Pelagian"—I didn't for a moment believe that human merit contributed to my salvation.

What accounts for these misunderstandings, misrepresentations, and accusations that often stop dialogue before it starts?

My wife and I learned years ago, the hard way, that it's a mistake to interpret each other's words as if they meant the same to each of us. Suppose one of us said, "If you want to, we could go out to dinner tonight."

The other might think this meant "I don't particularly want to, but if you do, I'll go" when in fact it meant "I *really do* want to go out."

Person A hears Person B's words and concludes, "If I said *that,* what I would mean is *this.*" Then B takes A's words to their logical conclusion (according to B's logic, not A's) and assumes that's what A actually believes. Much of the time, it isn't even close.

An Arminian says, "People have the freedom to choose as they wish." The Calvinist responds, "Oh, so you don't believe people have sin natures or that God is sovereign?" Shocked, the Arminian responds, "What? I believe in both!" The Calvinist insists, "No, you don't," because he doesn't understand that what to him are logical conclusions to the Arminian's statement are *not* logical conclusions to the Arminian.

> Any of us can "prove" nearly anything with some passages of Scripture, as long as we leave out *other* passages.

Similarly the Arminian hears the Calvinist say, "God elects people to salvation and empowers them to believe." The Arminian concludes, "Then you don't believe people have the ability to make choices; you think they're robots, and there's no point in evangelism and missions." In her mind, all these are perfectly logical conclusions to the Calvinist's statement. But they're not the Calvinist's conclusions.

When a Calvinist friend, believing that only Calvinists can have a big view of God, dismissed A. W. Tozer because he called himself a Calminian (half Calvinist, half Arminian), I encouraged him to read *The Knowledge of the Holy* and ask whether Tozer had a big view of God. To anyone who has actually read that remarkable book, it's a rhetorical question.

Tozer is one of those writers who bridges gaps between Bible-believers. I once had lunch with a Calvinist theologian and an Arminian theologian, both well known, and one of them asked me what book besides the Bible had the most impact on me. I responded, *"The Knowledge of the Holy."* The Calvinist said, "No kidding? Me too." The Arminian, stunned, said, "Exactly the book that most influenced me!"

Believing in the same Lord and the same Bible, Calvinists and Arminians have far more in common than not. Let's not dismiss the positions of thoughtful, Bible-believing people just because they think differently and use words differently. Any of us can "prove" nearly anything with some passages of Scripture, as long as we leave out *other* passages.

In terms of belief in the Bible and love for Christ, Calvinists and Arminians have a lot in common. Most Calvinists live daily as Arminians do—freely making choices for which they take personal responsibility. Most Arminians pray like Calvinists—believing a sovereign God can and does change people's hearts, swaying their wills.

There are better questions than "Are you a Calvinist or an Arminian?" One of those is "What does the Bible actually teach?" And "Do you believe it?" Let's trust all of God's words, not just the ones that fit neatly into a preferred theological system or church tradition. That's my approach in this book.

The Bible says a great deal about both God's control and our choices.

I'm aware the title of this book could frustrate people. The Calvinist may think *hand in Hand* sounds like the cooperative work of two equals, which glorifies man and insults God. Some may not notice it's the lowercase *h*and of humanity in the uppercase *H*and of God. God's hand controls far more than ours, and whenever he wishes, he can tighten or loosen his grip.

The Arminian could be frustrated by the fact that *hand in Hand* implies that human beings are like children, with the child's "choices" basically in the parent's complete control. I would point out that the child holding her parent's hand is still free to do things with her other hand.

Am I presumptuous enough to believe that this book will solve a puzzle so complex it was left hanging by brilliant theologians such as

Augustine, Calvin, Arminius, and Wesley? Absolutely not. But a question need not be *fully* resolved in order to have *some* light shed upon it.

It's good for us to let God's Word stretch our brains. Rather than frustrating, it can be enlightening and at times exhilarating.

You need to see the whole to get the most benefit from each part of this book.

No single chapter here is entirely balanced. Chapter 3 could be cited to prove I don't really believe in meaningful human choice, and chapter 4 to prove I don't believe in God's sovereignty. Before you draw firm conclusions, read both chapters and those that follow them. This book is not long, technical, or obscure. I've tried to cut to the heart of the issue, and I've therefore left many rabbit trails untraveled.

> Take a fresh look at Scripture; sometimes what it says is different from what you've been told.

I cite both Calvinists and Arminians. I'm not pretending their theologies aren't different; they obviously are, and some of the differences are important. What I'm doing is showing that people on both sides of the issue can sometimes make sense.

In one of my classes in Bible college, a theology professor spent days verbally tearing apart a newly released book which taught a view contrary to that held by the college. The book's arguments, as represented by my professor, were clearly unbiblical and laughably weak. I assumed my professor's criticisms were accurate, since he was a brilliant professor and a good man.

That summer I read that book for myself, and I found it to be an outstanding and fair-minded treatment of Scripture. Its message bore almost no resemblance to what the professor had dismantled in our classroom.

My appeal is for readers to have an open mind to other theological viewpoints when they're supported by God's Word. And take a fresh look at Scripture. Sometimes what it says is different from what you've been told it says.

Ask God to speak to you first and foremost through the Scriptures presented in each chapter.
God says, "So shall my word be that goes out from my mouth; it shall not return to me empty, but it shall accomplish that which I purpose, and shall succeed in the thing for which I sent it" (Isaiah 55:11, ESV). He says this not about your words or mine, but only his. So please, as you read this book:

- Reflect on God's Word more than you reflect on what I have to say about it.
- Be quick to measure my words by Scripture, like the Bereans who "examined the Scriptures every day to see if what Paul said was true" (Acts 17:11).

This will require discipline and a mind truly open to the revealed Word of God. But I believe if we carefully listen to all God has to say, he'll surprise us with the breadth, depth, and beauty of what he has revealed about both his sovereignty and our meaningful choice.

Notes

1. TULIP is an acronym representing Total depravity, Unconditional election, Limited atonement, Irresistible grace, and Perseverance of the saints. These "five points of Calvinism" were stated at the Synod of Dort in the early 1600s in response to five assertions of the Arminian "Remonstrants." See also chapter 2.
2. John Calvin, *Institutes of the Christian Religion,* ed. John T. McNeill (Louisville, KY: Westminster John Knox, 2006), 1:688.
3. C. H. Spurgeon, "Sovereign Grace and Man's Responsibility" (sermon 207, Royal Surrey Gardens, August 1, 1858), wwwspurgeon.org/sermons /0207.htm.
4. *The American Heritage Dictionary,* s.v. "Arminian," www.ahdictionary .com/word/search.html?q=Arminian.

5. Michael Marlowe, "What Is Arminianism?," Bible Research, www.bible-researcher.com/arminianism.html.

6. Robert E. Picirilli, *Grace, Faith, Free Will* (Nashville: Randall House, 2002), 41.

7. Bernardus, "De Libero Arbit. et Gratia," quoted in Jacob Arminius, *The Works of James Arminius, D.D.,* trans. James Nichols (Auburn, NY: Derby, Miller and Orton, 1853), 1:531.

8. *The American Heritage Dictionary,* s.v. "Calvinism," www.ahdictionary .com/word/search.html?q=Calvinism.

9. Tim Challies, "An Introduction to Calvinism and Arminianism," *Informing the Reforming* (blog), November 24, 2003, www.challies .com/articles/an-introduction-to-calvinism-arminianism.

10. Erwin Lutzer, *The Doctrines That Divide: A Fresh Look at the Doctrines That Separate Christians* (Grand Rapids, MI: Kregel, 1989), 212.

11. C. Michael Patton, "Twelve Myths About Arminianism," Credo House Ministries, *Parchment and Pen Blog,* August 8, 2013, www.reclaiming themind.org/blog/2013/08/twelve-myths-about-arminianism/.

12. Roger Olson, *Arminian Theology: Myths and Realities* (Downers Grove, IL: InterVarsity, 2006), 116.

13. David Servant, "Calvinism's Five Points Considered," Shepherd Serve, www.heavensfamily.org/ss/calvinism/calvinism-total-depravity-and -irresistible-grace.

14. F. L. Forlines, *Classical Arminianism: A Theology of Salvation,* ed. J. M. Pinson (Nashville: Randall House, 2011), 156.

15. Examples of four-pointers have included Puritan Richard Baxter, J. C. Ryle, and theologians Millard Erickson, Bruce Demarest, Bruce Ware, and Gregg Allison. Calvin sometimes appears to clearly affirm limited atonement, other times unlimited atonement. Calvin commented on Mark 14:24, that when Christ said he shed his blood for "many," "By the word *many* he means not a part of the world only, but the whole human race" (*Calvin's Commentaries,* "Commentary on Matthew, Mark, and Luke," vol. 3, www.ccel.org/ccel/calvin/calcom33 .ii.xxvii.html).

16. See R. C. Sproul video portion 2:35 to 2:45 at Nicholas Voss, "Men Who Think They Are Four Point Calvinists Are Actually No Point Calvinists," *Nicholas Voss* (blog), http://nickvoss.wordpress.com/2012/06/04/men-who -think-they-are-four-point-calvinists-are-actually-no-point-calvinists/.

17. "There are no Four-Point Calvinists," www.reformationtheology.com /2006/03/there_are_no_fourpoint_calvini_1.php.

18. Gary L. Shultz, *A Multi-Intentioned View of the Extent of the Atonement* (Eugene, OR: Wipf & Stock, 2014).

19. "Citations from Calvin on the unlimited work of expiation and redemption of Christ," http://calvinandcalvinism.com/?p=230.

20. Califgracer, "Notes on Calvinism: Calvinism, a Rigged Carnival Game," *Notes from a Retired Preacher* (blog), September 14, 2013, http:// expreacherman.com/2013/09/.

21. Dr. C. Matthew McMahon, "The 'god' of Arminianism Is Not Worshippable," *A Puritan's Mind* (blog), www.apuritansmind.com/arminianism /the-%E2%80%9Cgod%E2%80%9D-of-arminianism-is-not -worshippable/.

22. Daniel Jones, "Calvinism Is Evil," *The Usual Foolishness* (blog), February 21, 2014, http://usualfoolishness.com/2014/02/21/calvinism-is-evil/.

23. Marc D. Carpenter, "Are All Arminians Unsaved?," *Outside the Camp* (blog), www.outsidethecamp.org/efl161.htm.

24. William Chillingworth, *The Religion of Protestants: A Safe Way to Salvation* (London: George Bell, 1888), 423.

25. Dr. A. M. Hills, "Calvinism and Arminianism Compared," *Biblical Theology* (blog), www.biblical-theology.net/calvinism_and_arminianism _compared.htm.

26. Jerry Johnson, "Why Do Calvinist [sic] Believe Arminians Are Teaching Works Salvation?," Calvinism Is the Gospel, February 19, 2014, http:// calvinismisthegospel.com/why-do-calvinist-believe-arminians-are -teaching-works-salvation-by-jerry-johnson/#sthash.TyyBRUn4.dpuf.

27. Stephen Parker, "Reincarnation and Predestination," *Mystic444* (blog), October 17, 2009, http://mystic444.wordpress.com/page/16/.

28. Roger Olson, *Against Calvinism* (Grand Rapids, MI: Zondervan, 2011), 23.

3

The Sovereignty of God

I am God, and there is no other;
    I am God, and there is none like me,
declaring the end from the beginning
    and from ancient times things not yet done,
saying, "My counsel shall stand,
    and I will accomplish all my purpose."

Isaiah 46:9–10, ESV

Cheer up, Christian! Things are not left to chance:
no blind fate rules the world. God hath purposes,
and those purposes are fulfilled. God hath plans,
and those plans are wise, and never can be
dislocated.

Charles Spurgeon

In 1815 a confident Napoleon Bonaparte determined where and when to advance against the British. He chose Waterloo as the place and June 18 as the day, believing England would be at France's feet by battle's end. But it was not to be, and historians believe rain was one of the factors that dramatically affected the outcome.

Years later, French novelist Victor Hugo wrote, "Providence only required a little rain.... A cloud crossing the sky at a season when rain was not expected was sufficient to overthrow an empire."[1]

Victor Hugo had a biblical basis for his conjecture. The Bible tells of God sovereignly sending and withholding rain for his purposes in Leviticus 26:4; 1 Kings 8:35; 18:41–45; Isaiah 55:10; Jeremiah 5:24; 14:22; Zechariah 10:1; and James 5:17–18.

> Human arrogance daily makes foolish claims that beg to be disproven.

The prophet Jeremiah asked, "Are there any among the false gods of the nations that can bring rain? Or can the heavens give showers? Are you not he, O Lord our God? We set our hope on you, for you do all these things" (Jeremiah 14:22, esv).

Rain is a small thing, one of countless thousands of things in this universe that God can use to his ends, mostly in ways unknown to us.

I don't know whether the builder of the *Titanic* really said, "God himself couldn't sink this ship," but I do know that human arrogance daily makes foolish claims that beg to be disproven.

Many centuries before Napoleon, another arrogant ruler, Nebuchadnezzar, made a humbling discovery. God promised to take Nebuchadnezzar's kingdom from him for a time, and told him, "Your kingdom will be restored to you when you acknowledge that Heaven rules" (Daniel 4:26). That's exactly what happened, and the truly humbled king afterward insisted that God "does as he pleases with the powers of heaven and the peoples of the earth. No one can hold back his hand or say to him: 'What have you done?'" (verse 35).

Our God is sovereign.
Arminian theologian Jack Cottrell says, "The sovereignty of God may be concisely summed up as *absolute Lordship*. It is the same as the concept of kingdom or kingship or dominion."[2]

Calvinist theologian A. A. Hodge defined God's sovereignty as "His absolute right to govern and dispose of all his creatures simply according to his own good pleasure."[3]

I think nearly all Christians could agree with a definition of God's sovereignty that affirms all things are under God's rule and that nothing in the universe happens unless he either causes or permits it.

God's love, mercy, and grace, as well as his holiness, justice, and wrath, are all perfect. He is everywhere present, so that no place in the universe is beyond his reach, and no atom or molecule is astray. Therefore he cannot be frustrated, wishing he could do what he can't. Theologian Abraham Kuyper, who was also prime minister of the Netherlands, explained, "There is not a square inch in the whole domain of our human existence over which Christ, who is Sovereign over *all,* does not cry: 'Mine'!"[4]

"Dominion belongs to the LORD and he rules over the nations" (Psalm 22:28). Because God has absolute power, no one—including demons and humans who choose to violate his moral will—can thwart his ultimate purpose.

> God's sovereignty means he has ownership and authority over the entire universe.

Christ "upholds the universe by the word of his power" (Hebrews 1:3, ESV). The Greek word translated "upholds" is *phero,* "to carry," the same word used in Luke 5:18 when the friends of the paralyzed man carried him, on his sleeping mat, to Jesus for healing. God carries the entire universe as men carry a bed.

Paul wrote, "In him we were also chosen, having been predestined according to the plan of him who works out everything in conformity with the purpose of his will" (Ephesians 1:11). What does that "everything" include?

Arminian theologian Jack Cottrell says that in the context of Ephesians 1, that word "does not have a universal reference; God's purposive or decretive will does not include all things that happen in the whole scope of nature and history. It does include the establishment of the church, however, as the body which unites Jews and Gentiles under the one head, Jesus Christ (cf. 1:10)."5

Most Calvinists, on the other hand, interpret the "everything" in Ephesians 1:11 to be comprehensive, allowing for no exceptions, meaning that God works even in those things done against his moral will.

Countless biblical passages affirm God's sovereignty over human lives and circumstances.

Many verses make clear that though God's creatures can oppose him, they cannot ultimately prevail. For example:

> I make known the end from the beginning,
>   from ancient times, what is still to come.
> I say: My purpose will stand,
>   and I will do all that I please. (Isaiah 46:10)

> I know that the LORD is great,
>   that our Lord is greater than all gods.
> The LORD does whatever pleases him,
>   in the heavens and on the earth. (Psalm 135:5–6)

Our Creator is "God, the blessed and only Ruler, the King of kings and Lord of lords" (1 Timothy 6:15). The Bible says of him,

> You are the ruler of all things.
> In your hands are strength and power
>   to exalt and give strength to all. (1 Chronicles 29:12)

> He stands alone, and who can oppose him?
>   He does whatever he pleases. (Job 23:13)

> The Most High rules the kingdom of men and gives it to
>   whom he will. (Daniel 4:17, ESV)

Even what appears random is not: "The lot is cast into the lap, but its every decision is from the LORD" (Proverbs 16:33). Jesus said, "Are not two sparrows sold for a penny? And not one of them will fall to the ground apart from your Father. But even the hairs of your head are all numbered" (Matthew 10:29–30, ESV).

If we believe these things, our reaction to many of the difficulties we face will change. Problems will seem smaller, for although we can't control them, we know God can—and that everything will work out for his glory and our good.

God is sovereign over evil and disaster.

Though evil had no part in God's original creation, it was part of his original plan, because *redemption* from evil was part of his plan. Before he created the world, he knew evil would come and used it to play a necessary role in his redemptive plan.

Scripture doesn't distance God from disasters and secondary evils the way his children often do. Rather, he says unapologetically, "I form the light and create darkness, I bring prosperity and create disaster; I, the LORD, do all these things" (Isaiah 45:7). Amos 3:6 says, "When disaster comes to a city, has not the LORD caused it?" A description of natural disasters follows in Amos 4:6–12, where God says he intended these disasters not only as punishment but also as discipline designed to draw his people back to himself. (These passages have specific contexts in which God is bringing judgment on his people; they do *not* prove that all disasters are God's judgment.)

Even when Satan is behind natural disasters and diseases, God hasn't relinquished his world-governing power. Some emphasize that Satan, not God, brings natural disasters, inflicts diseases, orchestrates tragedies, and takes lives. And some passages appear to support that view, including those in the Gospels that link demon affliction with certain diseased people.

The book of Job draws back the curtain into the invisible realm, revealing how God and Satan relate in a case of great human adversity that included two natural disasters:

Then the LORD said to Satan, "Have you considered my servant Job? There is no one on earth like him; he is blameless and upright, a man who fears God and shuns evil."

"Does Job fear God for nothing?" Satan replied. "Have you not put a hedge around him and his household and everything he has?... But stretch out your hand and strike everything he has, and he will surely curse you to your face."

The LORD said to Satan, "Very well, then, everything he has is in your hands, but on the man himself do not lay a finger."

Then Satan went out from the presence of the LORD. (Job 1:8–12)

Satan incited the Sabeans to murder Job's servants and steal his oxen and donkeys (see verses 14–15). Then one of Job's servants reported, "The fire of God fell from the sky and burned up the sheep and the servants" (verse 16). Next, Chaldean raiding parties stole camels and murdered more servants (see verse 17). Finally, while Job's sons and daughters feasted in their oldest brother's house, a mighty wind caused the house to collapse, killing them all (see verses 18–19).

Were the Sabeans and Chaldeans responsible for committing the murders and thefts? Yes. Was Satan responsible for inciting them? Yes. He also brought about the severe lightning and gale-force winds.

Satan may bring about a "natural" disaster, but the book of Job makes clear that God continues to reign, even while selectively allowing Satan to do evil things. Satan knew that without God's explicit permission, he had no authority to incite humans to do evil, to bring down lightning to cause fires, or to send the wind to blow down a building and take lives. We should know this too.

Evil never takes God by surprise, nor makes him helpless.

The Bible calls Christ "the Lamb that was slain from the creation of the world" (Revelation 13:8). It also says God "chose us in him [Christ] before the creation of the world" (Ephesians 1:4) and that "He predestined us to be adopted through Jesus Christ for Himself, according to His favor and will" (verse 5, HCSB).

God intended for good the evil actions of Joseph's brothers, as well as Joseph's subsequent hard life in Egypt.
Joseph recognized God's sovereignty when he said to his brothers, who years before had sold him into slavery, "God sent me ahead of you to preserve for you a remnant on earth and to save your lives by a great deliverance. So then, it was not you who sent me here, but God" (Genesis 45:7–8). God not only permitted Joseph's journey to Egypt; he *sent* him there—through his brothers' evil deeds.

God isn't the author of evil, but he is the author of a story that includes evil.

Joseph also told his brothers, "As for you, you meant evil against me, but God meant it for good, to bring it about that many people should be kept alive, as they are today" (Genesis 50:20, ESV). "God meant it for good" communicates that God did not merely make the best of a bad situation; on the contrary, fully aware of what Joseph's brothers would do, and permitting their sin, God *intended* that the bad situation be used for good. While the brothers chose evil, God chose good. Both did as they chose, but God's choice triumphed. He chose to use their evil to bring about great good for Joseph's family as well as two nations—Israel and Egypt.

God isn't the author of evil, but he is the author of a story that includes evil. In his sovereignty, he intended from the beginning to permit evil, then to turn evil on its head and use it for a redemptive good. God didn't devise his redemptive plan on the fly, simply making the best of events that had spiraled out of his control.

An earlier passage from Genesis dramatically sets up chapter 50. God said to Abraham, "Know for certain that your offspring will be sojourners in a land that is not theirs and will be servants there, and they will be afflicted for four hundred years" (Genesis 15:13, ESV). God explained that he would bring Israel into the Promised Land to drive out the land's inhabitants exactly when Israel would be ready for deliverance and the Amorites would be ready for judgment (see verse 16).

Obviously, most of us who are Christ-followers aren't instruments to deliver God's chosen nation. But we still have much in common with Joseph. He was God's child; so are we. This is why I think it's fair to conclude that God didn't act out of character with Joseph. Certainly Joseph's large-scale impact was exceptional, but I believe God showed us in Joseph that he sovereignly works in *our* lives as well. What's remarkable isn't how dissimilar to Joseph's our lives are, but how similar—complete with tragic turns of events through which God can manifest his grace and accomplish his plans.

God is sovereign in the outworking of historical events, saying certain things "must" happen.

Jesus declared that some events "must" happen, in line with Scripture and God's sovereign will. Among them:

> From that time on Jesus began to explain to his disciples that he *must* go to Jerusalem and suffer many things at the hands of the elders, chief priests and teachers of the law, and that he *must* be killed and on the third day be raised to life. (Matthew 16:21)

> When you hear of wars and rumors of wars, do not be alarmed. Such things *must* happen, but the end is still to come. (Mark 13:7)

> And the gospel *must* first be preached to all nations. (Mark 13:10)

> But first he [the Son of Man] *must* suffer many things and be rejected by this generation. (Luke 17:25)

> Did not the Christ have to suffer these things and then enter his glory? (Luke 24:26)

Because of what the triune God knew and decided in eternity past, Jesus not only *might* or *could* go to the cross, but *had* to. God chose; his plan required what was sure to happen.

Peter, speaking to a Jerusalem crowd, said of Christ, "This man was handed over to you by God's set purpose and foreknowledge" (Acts 2:23).

God planned his redemptive work and did what was necessary to make it happen. The expressions "must happen," "must go to Jerusalem," "must die," and "set purpose" are the language of inevitability related to God's sovereign and predetermined purpose.

God is sovereign over disabilities and diseases.

In Scripture, physical afflictions are regarded sometimes as consequences of the Fall and sometimes as the work of demons, but they're ultimately seen as coming from God.

The Lord said to Moses, "Who gave man his mouth? Who makes him deaf or mute? Who gives him sight or makes him blind? Is it not I, the LORD?" (Exodus 4:11). Remarkably, *God* takes full "credit" for giving these disabilities. If disabilities, why not disorders and diseases? Are we to understand that God, through secondary means, also gives people Down syndrome, deformities, and cancer?

I may fail to understand it, but if the Bible is my authority, don't I have to believe it?

Every day since 1985 I've had to deal with the implications of my insulin-dependent diabetes. As a result, I recognize my absolute dependence on God. This has drawn me closer to him, and I'm deeply grateful.

Some Christians try to distance God from disabilities, arguing that if we attribute them to the sovereign hand of God, we're making him out to be a monster, causing people to resent him. This argument doesn't change what Exodus 4:11 actually says with startling clarity, that God directly *claims* to give people their disabilities. I may fail to understand it, but if the Bible is my authority, don't I have to believe it? I've spoken with many disabled people who didn't find comfort *until* they came to believe God made them as they are.

God uses disabilities to accomplish his unique purpose.
My brilliant friend David O'Brien has lived with a severe form of cerebral palsy since birth, and yet he demonstrates joy that transcends his body's bondage. David once asked me to join him at a conference for disabled people. He laboriously spoke what he'd written, then paused so I could read aloud every line.

David's message began, "Is it possible that God has his hand in shaping the events that could lead to a handicap or suffering?" Following David's notes, I read from Genesis 32:24–28, the story of Jacob wrestling with a man identified as God in human flesh. David observed, "We see Jacob's thigh touched by the Hand of God. Thereafter, his hip was out of joint. This handicap was caused directly by God's Hand." He continued, "I believe that the result of God's blessings [David called Jacob's handicap a blessing] were preservation of Jacob's life and a lifelong dependency upon God's ability to carry out his plan."

David spoke of God's affirmation in Exodus 4:11 that he *creates* people deaf, mute, and blind, and doesn't merely permit those conditions. Then he said, "God knows the spirit and will in each person, and he shapes the body to mold that will to his purpose. A gardener uses gradual tension to shape a tree into a beautiful arch. A special body is the gradual tension that shapes spirit and will to glorify God."

David then turned to John 9:1–3. The disciples wanted to attribute a man's blindness to human sin. Jesus corrected them: "Neither this man nor his parents sinned." Then Jesus stated the disability's purpose: "This happened *so that* the work of God might be displayed in his life." While God would receive great glory in the man's healing, surely he had a deliberate, divine purpose within the man's life, long before his healing. I think David O'Brien would agree that Satan, genetics, and many other things can serve as immediate or secondary causes, but God is still the ultimate and primary cause.

David commented, "If Christ had to suffer to be made complete, how can we expect not to have some form of suffering?" Then he said something unforgettable: "God tailors a package of suffering best suited for each of his own."

David spoke the following, in words difficult to understand, yet prophetically clear: "Dare I question God's wisdom in making me the way I am?"

Skeptics may say of disabled believers, "They're denying reality and finding false comfort. If there's a God who loves them, he wouldn't treat them like this."

David's audience found better reasons to believe and worship the sovereign God who purchased their resurrection with his blood—and who offers them comfort and perspective—than to believe the skeptics who've purchased nothing for them and offer only hopelessness.

God is sovereign in our own suffering.

Our state of mind determines whether the doctrine of God's sovereignty comforts or threatens us. In his nineteenth-century poem "Invictus," William Ernest Henley captured the proud human spirit. He spoke of his "unconquerable soul" and declared,

> It matters not how strait the gate,
> > How charged with punishments the scroll,
> I am the master of my fate;
> > I am the captain of my soul.[6]

Charles Spurgeon wrote, "There is no attribute of God more comforting to his children than the doctrine of Divine Sovereignty.... On the other hand, there is no doctrine more hated by worldlings."[7]

We don't want anyone, including God, to impose his way on us. James identified the arrogance of presuming we can do whatever we wish without submitting to God's plan:

> Now listen, you who say, "Today or tomorrow we will go to this
> or that city, spend a year there, carry on business and make
> money." Why, you do not even know what will happen tomor-
> row. What is your life? You are a mist that appears for a little
> while and then vanishes. (4:13–14)

Imagining that God should let us run life our way sets us up to resent God and even "lose our faith" when our lives don't go as we want. However, that's a faith we *should* lose—to be replaced with faith in the God of sovereign grace who doesn't *keep* us from all difficulties but promises to be *with* us in all difficulties.

We can trust God's loving sovereignty in every hardship.

Benjamin B. Warfield taught at Princeton Seminary for thirty-four years until his death in 1921. Students still read his books today yet few know his story. In 1876, at age twenty-five, he married Annie Kinkead. On their honeymoon, in an intense storm, lightning struck Annie and permanently paralyzed her. Warfield cared for her until she died in 1915. Because of her extreme needs, Warfield seldom left his home for more than two hours at a time during thirty-nine years of marriage.[8]

Warfield viewed his personal trials through the lens of Romans 8:28–29 and wrote this:

> The fundamental thought is the universal government of God. All that comes to you is under His controlling hand. The secondary thought is the favor of God to those that love Him. If He governs all, then nothing but good can befall those to whom He would do good.... And He will so govern all things that we shall reap only good from all that befalls us.[9]

Really, Dr. Warfield? *Only* good from *all* that befalls us? Warfield spoke from the playing field of suffering, answering an emphatic yes to the loving sovereignty of God.

Some believers have difficulty with God's involvement in orchestrating life's most difficult moments. Warfield viewed it very differently:

> It is because we cannot be robbed of God's providence that we know, amid whatever encircling gloom, that all things shall work together for good to those that love him.... Were not God's providence over all, could trouble come without his sending, were

Christians the possible prey of this or the other fiendish enemy, when perchance God was musing, or gone aside, or on a journey, or sleeping, what certainty of hope could be ours?... To suggest that it does not always come from his hands is to take away all our comfort.[10]

God has a way of making what seems worst into the very best.
Nancy Guthrie tells how a speaker once asked people to fold a piece of paper in half. She then instructed them to write on the top half the worst things that had happened to them, and on the bottom half the best things.[11]

Invariably, people find things at the top of the page that they also include at the bottom. Experiences they labeled as the worst things that had ever happened to them had, over time, given birth to some of the best things.

It's the same with my list. Try making your own. If enough time has passed since some of those "worst things" have happened, then almost certainly you'll find an overlap.

Our lists provide persuasive proof that while evil and suffering are not good, God can use them to accomplish immeasurable good. Knowing this should give us great confidence that even when we don't see any redemptive meaning in our present suffering, God can see it...and one day so will we.

We can agree that God is sovereign and all-powerful without agreeing about how he chooses to exercise his power.
God is "the LORD, strong and mighty, the LORD, mighty in battle!" (Psalm 24:8, ESV). The rhetorical question "Is anything too hard for the LORD?" implies the answer no (Genesis 18:14; compare Jeremiah 32:27). Gabriel said to Mary, "Nothing is impossible with God" (Luke 1:37). Jesus said, "With God all things are possible" (Matthew 19:26).

God is the "Almighty" (2 Corinthians 6:18; Revelation 1:8). He is "able to do far more abundantly than all that we ask or think" (Ephesians

3:20, ESV). John the Baptist said, "God is able from these stones to raise up children for Abraham" (Matthew 3:9, ESV).

God's sovereignty is real, but not every statement people make about it is true. Scripture emphasizes God's sovereignty, yet it fully recognizes the role of evil people as well as Satan and demons.

Scripture makes clear that Satan and demons in fact have a powerful influence on the course of events in this world (see 2 Thessalonians 2:9; 1 Timothy 4:1; 1 John 5:19; Revelation 12:9). An emphasis on God's sovereignty should not undermine or negate horrible evils.

In a sovereignty-only perspective, human choice can become buried so deep that it's nominal, essentially an illusion. "Since God is sovereign, it really doesn't matter how we live. Even if I choose sin, it will be according to God's plan. Why should I work hard at my job, my marriage, or my parenting when my effort doesn't matter and it's all in God's hands?" Yet Scripture is full of verses that contradict such a conclusion. When Moses said in Deuteronomy 30:19, "Choose life in order that you may live" (NASB), surely he wasn't saying, "God has predetermined all your choices, so although you *imagine* you're choosing, it's really God making you choose rightly or wrongly."

When Joshua said, "Choose this day whom you will serve" (Joshua 24:15, ESV), didn't he mean they *really* could choose, and that whether they chose either idols or God, it was genuinely their choice? We should of course call upon God to empower us to make right choices. But that's not the same as calling on God to make our decisions *for* us.

What about the many passages of Scripture that show the tragic results of sin? When Achan's sin resulted in the death of his family (see Joshua 7:10–26) and when Herod killed children in an attempt to murder Christ (see Matthew 2:16–18)—were these not real choices which God permitted and used, and in that sense determined—but which he did *not* determine in the sense of causing anyone to sin?

No Calvinist pastor says to his congregation, "Your choices don't matter, since God has sovereignly predetermined everything, including your sins and your Arminian theology!"

No, he admonishes his people to repent and avoid sin, and to change their theology by *choosing* to believe something different. Doesn't every sermon call on people to make good choices? And aren't most of those choices ones that can actually be made?

"His divine power has given us everything we need for life and godliness through our knowledge of him who called us by his own glory and goodness" (2 Peter 1:3). God has given all of us the capacity to make right choices; doesn't the fact that we often make wrong ones suggest that we, as well as God, are involved in determining our life direction?

God's sovereignty is affirmed emphatically, yet it doesn't swallow up our ability to choose or our responsibility for the choices we make. This leads us to our second major subject—meaningful human choice.

Notes

The second epigraph is from C. H. Spurgeon, "A Basket of Summer Fruit" (sermon 343, New Park Street Pulpit, Exeter Hall, the Strand, October 28, 1860), www.spurgeon.org/sermons/0343.htm.

1. Victor Hugo, *Les Misérables* (New York: Modern Library, 1992), 14.
2. Jack Cottrell, *What the Bible Says About God the Ruler* (Eugene: College Press Publishing, 2000), 266.
3. A. A. Hodge, *Outlines of Theology,* ed. William H. Goold (London: T. Nelson, n.d.), 130.
4. Abraham Kuyper, *Abraham Kuyper: A Centennial Reader,* ed. James D. Bratt (Grand Rapids, MI: Eerdmans, 1998), 461.
5. Jack Cottrell, "Dr. Jack Cottrell on Ephesians 1:1–11," *Arminian Today* (blog), http://arminiantoday.com/2012/10/03/dr-jack-cottrell-on-ephesians-11-11/.
6. William Ernest Henley, "Invictus," quoted in *101 Famous Poems,* comp. Roy J. Cook (Chicago: McGraw-Hill, 1958), 95.
7. C. H. Spurgeon, "Divine Sovereignty" (sermon 77, New Park Street Chapel, Southwark, May 4, 1856), www.spurgeon.org/sermons/0077.htm.
8. John D. Woodbridge, *Great Leaders of the Christian Church* (Chicago, Moody, 1989), 344.

9. B. B. Warfield, *Faith and Life* (Edinburgh: Banner of Truth, 1991), 20.

10. B. B. Warfield, "God's Providence over All," *Selected Shorter Writings,* ed. John E. Meeter (1929; repr. Grand Rapids, MI: Baker, 1991), 1:110.

11. Nancy Guthrie, *Holding On to Hope: A Pathway Through Suffering to the Heart of God* (Carol Stream, IL: Tyndale, 2002), 39.

4

Free Will and Meaningful Choice

Choose this day whom you will serve, whether the gods your fathers served in the region beyond the River, or the gods of the Amorites in whose land you dwell. But as for me and my house, we will serve the LORD.

Joshua 24:15, ESV

I wear the chain I forged in life.... I made it link by link, and yard by yard; I girded it on of my own free will, and of my own free will I wore it.

Jacob Marley's ghost, in *A Christmas Carol,* Charles Dickens

Seventy-six-year-old Liviu Librescu taught aerospace engineering at Virginia Tech. On April 16, 2007, when a homicidal gunman tried to enter his classroom, Librescu managed to barricade the door, giving all but one of his twenty students time to escape out the window. The killer shot Librescu five times. The final shot to his head killed him.

A Holocaust survivor, Librescu chose to stand between his students and a mass murderer, giving his life for them on, of all days, Holocaust Remembrance Day.

Librescu made a free and meaningful choice that saved his students' lives.

Both Arminians and Calvinists daily recognize the reality of human choice.

It may seem strange to you to read this treatment concerning human choice, since to you choice is likely self-evident, something you take for granted without ever thinking about it. But it's one of the two central subjects of this book, and it's important enough to deserve careful thought.

> That I chose to write this book—and you chose to read it—is compelling evidence of meaningful choice.

Some Arminians think that Calvinists disbelieve in human choice—hence the jokes about Calvinists being confused at a buffet when told they can choose whatever they want. In reality, just as most Arminians believe in God's sovereignty, so most Calvinists believe in real human choice.

Every time a Calvinist tries to convince an Arminian he's right, the Calvinist exercises his choice and calls upon the Arminian to do so—just as surely as every time an Arminian prays that God will change a Calvinist's mind, he acknowledges God sometimes interferes with human choice. That I chose to write this book—and you chose to read it—is compelling evidence of meaningful choice.

Arminians believe God sovereignly permits people to commit evil. People really can be victimized by other people; every murder, rape, and genocide proves this. Many Arminians believe that to suggest God has a plan in evil is to essentially blame God for the bad choices of his creatures.

Calvinists see God as permitting the same evil, but they use language stronger than permission: he does not cause evil, but "decrees" or "ordains" evil. He does this with a sovereign plan, even when we can see no good reason for a baby dying at childbirth or a terrible accident paralyzing someone for life. Calvinists believe that if God doesn't have such a plan, he isn't really in control. Many Arminians believe God's plan is not as wrapped up in all of life's details, including suffering, but is painted with a broader brush, in which creature choices determine much that God does not.

God gave humanity a choice even though he knew what that choice would be.

Choice is a function of someone's will. God has a will, and so do we. Satan also has a will, one opposed to God's (see 2 Timothy 2:26). A will is the property of any intelligent being, and the ability to choose is a central aspect of personhood.

God is intelligent, creative, communicative, and free to choose. So in practical terms, what does it mean to be made in his "likeness"? (See Genesis 1:27; 5:1.) While scholars debate the question, being made in God's image likely includes having some of his attributes, though on a finite level. We think because he thinks, we speak because he speaks, we create because he creates, and we choose because he chooses.

From the beginning, God knew what choices both angels and humans would make under what circumstances, and while he could have intervened to stop them from sinning, he wanted them to choose freely. To be preprogrammed is in keeping with a robot's nature, but not a human being's.

Philosopher Alvin Plantinga said, "God can create free creatures, but He can't cause or determine them to do only what is right."[1] Plantinga didn't mean God lacks the *power* to make his creatures do whatever he wants. He meant simply that if God uses that power to cause them to do whatever he wants, then his creatures cannot be called "free."

In *Mere Christianity*, C. S. Lewis wrote,

God created things which had free will. That means creatures which can go either wrong or right. Some people think they can imagine a creature which was free but had no possibility of going wrong; I cannot. If a thing is free to be good it is also free to be bad. And free will is what has made evil possible. Why, then, did God give them free will? Because free will, though it makes evil possible, is also the only thing that makes possible any love or goodness or joy worth having. A world of automata—of creatures that worked like machines—would hardly be worth creating. The happiness which God designs for His higher creatures is the happiness of being freely, voluntarily united to Him and to each other.... And for that they must be free.[2]

Lewis added this important point:

Of course God knew what would happen if they used their freedom the wrong way: apparently, He thought it worth the risk.... If God thinks this state of war in the universe a price worth paying for free will—that is, for making a live world in which creatures can do real good or harm and something of real importance can happen, instead of a toy world which only moves when He pulls the strings—then we may take it [that] it is worth paying.[3]

Adam and Eve freely chose to sin.
Genesis 2:16–17 tells us, "And the Lord God commanded the man, 'You are free to eat from any tree in the garden; but you must not eat from the tree of the knowledge of good and evil, for when you eat of it you will surely die.'"

We should take God's words at face value: "*You are free* to eat from any tree." Perhaps hundreds of trees filled Eden, but God forbade eating from only one. The biblical narrative would be nonsensical if God *required*

Adam and Eve to make a sinful choice. Satan influenced them but did not control them. They chose to exert their own will against God's.

God in his sovereignty certainly could and did orchestrate aspects of the circumstances under which sin entered the world. He could have chosen to forbid nothing. He could have made the fruit unattractive. He could have kept the devil out of the garden. He could have kept temptation away from them and could have kept them from falling. But he didn't.

This is very different from saying God actually *caused* them to sin. That would make God actively involved in the violation of his own command. It would also make God unjust, for if he forced Adam and Eve to sin, how could he hold them accountable for it? Scripture says God does not tempt anyone (see James 1:13).

God said to Eve, "What is this you have done?" (Genesis 3:13), not, "What did Satan make you do?" or "What did I cause you to do?" Adam, Eve, and Satan all made real choices—and God judged them accordingly.

On the one hand, God is not the author of evil, and did not make Adam and Eve sin. He was, however, the author of his creatures' capacity to choose between good and evil. And he was the author of circumstances in which he knew they would exercise their freedom to do evil. His creatures chose freely to sin, yet God didn't surrender his sovereignty for a moment.

> God could have made the forbidden fruit unattractive...but he didn't.

C. S. Lewis said that God "commands us to do slowly and blunderingly what He could do perfectly and in the twinkling of an eye. He allows us to neglect what He would have us do, or to fail. Perhaps we do not fully realize the problem, so to call it, of enabling finite free wills to co-exist with Omnipotence. It seems to involve at every moment almost a sort of divine abdication."[4]

Lewis's word "seems" is well chosen. He knew that a sovereign God doesn't abdicate his throne. However, his creation of meaningful human choice has surely complicated what could otherwise be a simple and straightforward sovereignty in which all God's creatures would do whatever God wants. To be sovereign in a world where his creatures regularly rebel against him and violate his will is a far greater challenge, requiring a far greater God.

The term *free will* is potentially misleading.

You may have noticed that I chose (freely) not to use the term *free will* in the subtitle of this book. Instead I speak of "meaningful choice." Why? Because I've witnessed discussions which demonstrate how the term *free will* inhibits communication and keeps common beliefs off the table.

I don't like the term *free will* because it can convey an inaccurate impression. Our wills have serious limitations. First, our free will is limited because we're finite. Even when morally perfect, Adam and Eve did not have the freedom to choose to fly or to make themselves taller or shorter. God alone is infinite and has completely free will that permits him to do whatever he wants (always in keeping with his flawless character).

In a world of cause and effect, even our small choices are influenced by people, circumstances, and events. Your "free will" concerning what shirt you buy at the sporting goods store could be affected by the weather, inventory, price range, what's on sale, your style preference (influenced by your older brother or the salesperson), and the fact that you grew up where people loved the Cowboys and hated the Giants.

However, our "free will" has more serious limitations due to our sin natures. *We are not just finite; we are fallen.* Jesus said, "I tell you the truth, everyone who sins is a slave of sin" (John 8:34, NLT). A slave is not free.

Calvin said, "How few men are there, I ask, who when they hear free will attributed to man do not immediately conceive him to be master of both his own mind and will, able of his own power to turn himself toward either good or evil."[5] He wrote, "Free will is not sufficient to enable man to do good works, unless he be helped by grace."[6]

Redeemed sinners, however, "have been set free from sin and have become slaves to God" (Romans 6:22). Therefore we have *freed* wills—that is, we can do right. But even redeemed sinners are not entirely free from sin, nor are we free to overcome our "flesh," or tendency toward sin-oriented human effort, without the grace and power of Christ (see Romans 8:1–4; Titus 2:11–12).

I believe we do have the ability to consider the options in front of us and make voluntary choices that have real effects. This is what I'm calling "meaningful choice." So if that's what you think *free will* means, then yes, I believe in it.

But I don't believe in free will as defined by evangelist Charles Finney: "Free-will implies the power of originating and deciding our own choices, and of exercising our own sovereignty, in every instance of choice upon moral questions—of deciding or choosing in conformity with duty or otherwise in all cases of moral obligation."[7]

I especially resist the expression "exercising our own sovereignty." Our freedom to choose "in conformity with duty" and "in *all* cases of moral obligation" suggests more than the human condition allows by indicating we have a capacity to make righteous choices, to the point that we could contend we don't ever sin. John says, "If we claim we have not sinned, we make [God] out to be a liar and his word has no place in our lives" (1 John 1:10).

Contrary choice, depending on how it is defined, may be a part of meaningful choice.

The term *contrary choice* used by Arminians is often opposed by Calvinists on the grounds that it implies that a sinner is capable of acting contrary to his sin nature. This, I believe, is a valid criticism. If *contrary choice* is intended to imply that human beings can thwart God's decree through their choices, I also disagree. God is said to have used Herod, Pilate, Gentiles, and Jews "to do whatever [his] hand and [his] plan had predestined to take place" (Acts 4:28, ESV). Did Herod and Pilate and the others have sufficient contrary choice to have acted differently to the extent that they could have thwarted God's plan? Clearly not.

Sometimes contrary choice is rejected because it's thought to imply

God can't know what will happen if, at the moment of making a choice, a person might make a different one; but surely God can know all the choices a person could have made or nearly made, as well as the only one a person actually will make. While some will argue that determinism means only one choice is possible, compatibilism holds that determinism and free choice can coexist. Isn't the mind of God big enough to determine some things or many things while granting genuine choice to his creatures? If *contrary choice* simply implies the existence of more than one possible choice, isn't that what *choice* means in the first place? If our view of God is sufficiently large, this kind of contrary choice is no threat to his sovereignty.

In the philosophy of libertarianism, *contrary choice* is often associated with human autonomy, a word that means self-government and freedom from outside influence. Viewed that way, contrary choice would be contrary to God's sovereignty. However, setting it aside as a technical term, don't most of us believe in what could be called contrary choice? Don't we believe that those without Christ can choose to go to work or stay home (each a contrary choice to the other), or choose not to rob a bank rather than rob it? And that those in Christ can call upon the Holy Spirit to help them resist temptation and remain faithful to their spouse? In resisting temptation, don't we always make a contrary choice—one that's different from the choice made if we'd given in to the temptation?

Call this "contrary choice," "different choice," or "real choice," it seems hard to distinguish from just plain choice. I'm aware that some people load far more meaning, and different meanings, into the term *contrary choice.* My recommendation is, if you are discussing it with someone, rather than embracing or outright rejecting it, define the term carefully and explain what you reject and what you can accept. As with *free will,* you will either agree or disagree not automatically, but depending on what is actually meant.

If someone believes contrary choice means the freedom to choose contrary to God's decree, I obviously disagree. If it means that when you hand me a fruit bowl I can choose a banana rather than an apple, or that after my choice I can look back and say I *could have* chosen the apple instead, I don't see that as problematic to God's sovereign determination to accomplish his purposes.

If contrary choice doesn't magnify me as though I were a god but simply means I can, by my God-created nature or by the common or special grace of God, choose one option instead of another, then in most cases I affirm that to be true. Every day I make hundreds of choices, just as I did every day before I came to know Christ. If they're truly choices, then I could have, within limitations, made different choices—and had I done so, God wouldn't have ever been surprised.

Scripture itself regularly calls upon me to make different choices, to choose purity over impurity, to choose love, peace, and encouragement and to choose against (in contrary choice) hate, bitterness, gossip, and lust. By God's grace and empowerment, I can, in that sense, make these contrary choices.

God commands us to "put off your old self...and to be renewed in the spirit of your minds, and to put on the new self, created after the likeness of God in true righteousness and holiness" (Ephesians 2:22–24, ESV). It tells us to "put away falsehood" and "speak the truth," "be angry and do not sin" (verses 25–26). It commands the thief to "no longer steal" and to instead "labor, doing honest work" (verse 28). Don't each of these commands represent contrary choices that God says I can and should, by his grace, make?

Cannot unbelievers, by God's common grace, do acts of kindness to help the poor and needy, and choose to be faithful to their spouse and to love their children rather than be unfaithful and unloving?

In doing such things, don't all people exercise a form of contrary choice by doing one thing when they could instead have done another? In my opinion, Calvinists sometimes argue too strongly against the notion of contrary choice. Yes, we should insist there is no contrary choice if it means playing God, utter autonomy, or acting contrary to one's nature. People don't choose devoid of a nature, disposition, prior influence, prejudice, or inclination. Neither can they violate God's sovereign decree.

In the limited sense I've stated above, though, I don't see the problem with a Calvinist affirming contrary choice.

Who can choose meaningfully?

Having addressed the limits of human free will, we should recognize that the Bible on nearly every page assumes human beings have the ability to make meaningful choices, which includes choosing one thing instead of another.

Literally thousands of examples could be given. For instance, Paul wrote, "Each one must give as he has decided in his heart, not reluctantly or under compulsion, for God loves a cheerful giver" (2 Corinthians 9:7, ESV). Note that the extent of our choices includes attitudes as well as actions. Choosing to give *cheerfully* may involve a process of renewing our minds (see Romans 12:1–2), which requires a work of God's Spirit, but it's a work we can choose to ask for, accept, and freely participate in.

Look up all the Bible verses containing some form of the word *choose* and you'll find that a remarkable number of them speak of God's choices. *His* free will dominates Scripture. But God's Word regularly speaks of humans making meaningful choices—choosing what to believe and whether to love God and love people, as well as countless other choices.

After God set forth his laws to Israel and laid out the consequences for obedience and disobedience, Moses assured his fellow Israelites, "Now what I am commanding you today is *not too difficult for you or beyond your reach*" (Deuteronomy 30:11). They had a choice. Therefore Moses said, "Choose life,…love the LORD your God, listen to his voice, and hold fast to him" (verses 19–20).

Centuries later, God told his people, "I take no pleasure in the death of the wicked, but rather that they turn from their ways and live. Turn! Turn from your evil ways! Why will you die, O house of Israel?" (Ezekiel 33:11). Would God make such an emotional, heartfelt plea to those who had no choice except to refuse him?

Consider Proverbs 4:13–15: "Hold on to instruction, do not let it go; guard it well, for it is your life. Do not set foot on the path of the wicked or walk in the way of evil men. Avoid it, do not travel on it; turn from it and go on your way." Some will choose to obey these commands; some will not. Are those choices real and meaningful so that all will be held accountable for them? Yes.

Any view of God's sovereignty and human choice that doesn't include a real and true human ability to choose undermines not only many specific passages of Scripture but also the nature of God's Word. Yes, there are certain commands we don't have the power to fulfill: "Be perfect, even as your Father in heaven is perfect" (Matthew 5:48, NLT). But hundreds of commands in the book of Proverbs, many of them behavioral, some attitudinal, contain examples that even unbelievers have the freedom to perform.

> Scripture calls human beings to choose and continuously describes them as making choices.

True, God's law fulfills the role of showing us we cannot fully obey, and we will fall short (see Romans 3:20, 23). But when it comes, for instance, to God's commands to use honest scales and not cheat one's customers (see Leviticus 19:36; Proverbs 16:11), millions of unbelievers have proven they are, through their God-informed consciences and his common grace, capable of obeying.

Augustine and Pelagius debated free will.

The first known free-will debate was between Augustine and Pelagius, in the late fourth century. Pelagius was not orthodox and therefore is not to be equated with Bible-believing Arminians. Rather, he was more like today's liberal Christian denominations that no longer believe the teachings of Scripture. A British monk, Pelagius vehemently opposed the first part of Augustine's prayer, "Grant what Thou commandest, and command what Thou dost desire."

What Augustine meant was that God must bestow his grace on people to enable them to do what he commands. Pelagius hated this idea, believing that responsibility implies ability. If a person can be held morally accountable to obey God's law, then fairness demands that he has the ability to obey without special empowerment.

Pelagius believed God has given people freedom to choose one way or another, and they need nothing more from God in order to make their choices.

He also denied that all people sinned in Adam, as explicitly taught in Romans 5:18–19: "the result of one trespass was condemnation for all men...through the disobedience of the one man the many were made sinners." Pelagius taught that children come into the world with the same innocence of the pre-Fall Adam and Eve. Today, the beliefs of Pelagius are widespread in liberal churches. The Pelagian position is more appealing and less insulting to people than the Pauline position, but the issue for Bible-believers is not which position sounds most fair but which is biblically true.

The core conflict between Augustine and Pelagius was not only the doctrine of original sin but the question of how free human beings really are.

Again, orthodox Arminianism is not inherently Pelagian or semi-Pelagian, but any individual person may be either. That's why it's important to understand the historic debate and the different meanings behind the words.

Luther and Erasmus debated free will in a way that helped define the Reformation.

In 1524, Desiderius Erasmus wrote *On Free Will* to refute Martin Luther's teachings. In response, Martin Luther penned *On the Bondage of the Will*. Their exchange remains lively and current because although culture has changed, the issues have not.

Theologian Roger Olson says, "Arminius and his faithful followers...were also influenced by the Catholic reformer Erasmus."[8] Olson also says that Arminians believe that "in salvation, God's grace is the superior partner; human free will (nonresistance) is the lesser partner."[9] This corresponds to Erasmus's view. Luther, in contrast, would likely reply, "Human free will cannot be any partner at all in salvation, because those who are dead have no power to participate in their own resurrection."

Luther believed that people do indeed willingly receive salvation in

Christ, but he also believed that God must give them spiritual life to make their wills responsive. Erasmus would disagree, saying that God has given each person sufficient free will to make an intelligent choice whether to come to Christ.

> Luther emphasized the human need for God's grace and empowerment to obey.

Luther believed that only when God brings new birth to an individual does that person receive power to love God instead of sin. But Luther clarified his belief in free will in matters that didn't accompany salvation: "Free choice is allowed to man only with respect to what is beneath him.... In relation to God, or in matters pertaining to salvation or damnation, a man has no free choice, but is a captive."[10]

Erasmus believed God wouldn't command us to do something we're incapable of; Luther viewed God's commands as a measuring standard to show us our inability to choose righteously.

Grace alone saves us, Luther maintained, and God's empowering us to choose righteously comes to us only with his saving grace. While affirming God's grace, Erasmus believed that repenting and turning from sin to God was within the power of human free choice. Luther supposedly said to Erasmus (and if he didn't say it, he should have), "When you are finished with all your commands and exhortations...I'll write Romans 3:20 over the top of it all."

Why did Luther believe this single verse ended the argument? Because it says observing the law will not impart righteousness *since no one will observe the law.*

Because God repeatedly commands us to obey him, Erasmus argued, we *must* have the capacity to do so. Erasmus's argument appears to make sense. After all, Nanci and I never commanded our children to levitate, but we did tell them to stay away from drugs.

Luther argued that even schoolboys know that when commands are used, "nothing else is signified than that which *ought* to be done," which is different than saying it can be done.[11] In other words, *ought* and *able* are not the same.

The Reformation is typically understood to have centered on the doctrine of justification. Yet that doctrine was inseparable from the issue of God's sovereignty and the extent and power of human free will.

Does the Arminian belief in free will mean God is not sovereign?

Arminian theologian Roger Olson wrote,

> The only thing the Arminian view of God's sovereignty necessarily excludes is God's authorship of sin and evil. Faithful followers of Arminius have always believed that God governs the entire universe and all of history. Nothing at all can happen without God's permission, and many things are specifically and directly controlled and caused by God. Even sin and evil do not escape God's providential governance in classical Arminian theology. God permits and limits them without willing or causing them.[12]

On the other hand, many Arminians believe that Calvinists think human beings have *no* capacity to choose. R. C. Sproul disagreed with this, saying,

> Augustine did not deny that fallen man still has a will and that the will is capable of making choices.... We still are able to choose what we desire, but our desires remain chained by our evil impulses. He argued that the freedom that remains in the will always leads to sin. Thus in the flesh we are free only to sin, a hollow freedom indeed.... True liberty can only come from without, from the work of God on the soul. Therefore we are not only partly dependent upon grace for our conversion but totally dependent upon grace.[13]

When sinners come to Christ, they take on Christ's righteousness, and the indwelling Holy Spirit empowers them. They're now free and capable of choosing to obey God. Without redemption, they have no freedom to do anything that makes them holy.

Calvin said, "We allow that man has choice and that it is self-determined, so that if he does anything evil, it should be imputed to him and to his own voluntary choosing. We do away with coercion and force, because this contradicts the nature of will and cannot coexist with it."[14]

Given the biblical teaching about our bondage to sin, *free will* may be a less helpful term than Augustine's "reasonable self-determination."

Wayne Grudem, a five-point Calvinist, explains, "We think about what to do, consciously decide what we will do, and then we follow the course of action that we have chosen.... Our choices really do determine what will happen. It is not as if events occur *regardless* of what we decide or do, but rather that they occur *because of* what we decide and do."[15]

Any Arminian will agree with that statement. God grants people choices that "really do determine what will happen." God has sovereignly determined that our choices will *truly* determine certain outcomes.

Free will and *total depravity* can be misleading.

Paul said of unbelievers, "They demonstrate that God's law is written in their hearts, for their own conscience and thoughts either accuse them or tell them they are doing right" (Romans 2:15, NLT). To say that no sinner can save himself by doing good is not the same as saying no sinner is ever able to do good. An unbeliever who falls on a grenade to save the lives of children has certainly done something good.

The term *total depravity* never made sense to me, because it suggests "completely evil." I knew that my once notoriously anti-Christian father was sometimes kind, and faithfully provided for our family. No one sins all the time—even unregenerate people can make good choices. Can an unbelieving alcoholic stay sober? Absolutely. As recovery groups demonstrate, millions of unbelievers have learned to make choices contrary to their temptations. We're sinners, of course. But if we were all as depraved as we could be—*totally* depraved—human society couldn't exist.

I eventually came to realize that what Calvinists, and some Arminians (including John Wesley), call "total depravity" really means "total inability" to work our way to God's favor. Calvinist theologian Anthony Hoekema replaced "total depravity" with "pervasive depravity." His point is that sin pervades every part of our being and limits our range of choices. Arminians agree with Calvinists that apart from God's grace, sinners could never choose to receive Christ.

Unbelievers can modify sinful behaviors, but they can't escape the sin built into their nature or earn their way to Heaven. While Romans 7 says that sinners can't stop doing evil, it doesn't say they can never do good.

Arminians should agree that since people are slaves to sin, there are surely better terms to use than *free will*. A slave to sin is *not* free to make consistently righteous choices. Bible-believing Calvinists should agree that since unbelievers are capable of doing some things that aren't evil, *total depravity* is also a misleading term.

Meanwhile, if we're to have fruitful discussions, we need to refrain from boxing people in by taking *their* terms and applying to them *our* definitions. A Calvinist who believes in "total depravity" isn't saying that all people are as evil as they could possibly be. An Arminian who affirms "free will" is not necessarily denying that people are slaves to sin. We need to ask each other what we mean and not draw hasty conclusions.

Arminians can believe in total depravity, and Calvinists can believe in free will; it's all in the definitions.
A famous Reformer made the following statement. See if you can guess who it was:

> In this [fallen] state, the free will of man towards the true good is not only wounded, maimed, infirm, bent, and weakened; but it is also imprisoned, destroyed, and lost. And its powers are not only debilitated and useless unless they be assisted by grace, but it has no powers whatever except such as are excited by Divine grace. For Christ has said, "Without me ye can do nothing."[16]

So who said it? A good guess would be John Calvin. The correct guess would be Jacob Arminius.

In the third of their Remonstrant Articles of 1610, the early Arminians affirmed,

> That man does not have saving grace of himself, nor of the energy of his free will, inasmuch as he, in the state of apostasy and sin, can of and by himself neither think, will, nor do anything that is truly good (such as saving faith eminently is); but that it is needful that he be born again of God in Christ.[17]

Two prominent modern Arminians build on this language, saying,

> Human beings are not able to think, will, nor do anything good in and of themselves, including merit favor from God, save ourselves from the judgment and condemnation of God that we deserve for our sin, or even believe the gospel.... If anyone is to be saved, God must take the initiative.[18]

Calvinist Jonathan Edwards defined *free will* as "the ability to choose as one pleases." He explained, "A man never, in any instance, wills anything contrary to his desires, or desires anything contrary to his will."[19] In that sense, a sinner has unrestrained free will. But given his sinful nature, he's not free to desire everything, including true righteousness.

Though their theologies were very different in many areas, Jacob Arminius believed in human depravity and that man cannot will saving faith, while Jonathan Edwards believed in free will. Each man defined these terms as they understood them, so people knew what they meant. Those who discuss the issues today should do the same. That way we'll know when we mean different things when we use the same words, just as sometimes we mean the same things when using different words.

"Restricted choice" is not the same as "no choice."
Some affirm what seems a far too expansive free will. The moral condition of fallen humans, addictions, and other dominant influences can greatly diminish our volitional freedom.

Treatises on free will sometimes emphasize that no one can predict future choices. Those who understand addictions know an addict's future choices are very predictable, apart from making radical changes. The alcoholic will drink, the meth addict will take meth, the pornography addict, given the opportunity, will look at pornography (unless he has a compelling reason not to), Likewise, a pastry addict won't turn down a doughnut.

> We are free enough to be morally accountable, to make consequential choices—yet not free enough to make ourselves righteous before God.

Our addictions, desires, need for approval, and vulnerability to peer pressure may turn what appears to be a free choice into a "forced choice." We may make free choices uncoerced by any external force, but powerful internal urges may compel certain choices. In the absence of an external constraint, sinners will normally choose to sin. They don't *have* to do so; under threat of instant death, they could and likely would refrain. (Of course, people sometimes choose to drink and drive, knowing they may kill themselves and others; so while they *could* make the right choice, they *do* make the wrong one, sometimes repeatedly and therefore predictably.)

While we may—with effort and assistance—modify certain behaviors, and even some attitudes, Scripture reminds us we cannot, on our own, alter our fundamental nature. There's hope in Christ, who promises that the truth will set us free (see John 8:32). But before moving to freedom, we must come to grips with our bondage apart from Christ.

Jeremiah 17:9 says, "The heart is deceitful above all things, and desperately sick" (ESV). We're not innocent beings inclined to choose whatever's best. We're not even morally neutral beings. We're congenitally corrupt.

So how free are we, really? Free enough to be morally accountable, free enough to make consequential choices—yet not free enough to make ourselves righteous before God.

Wesley believed God extends prevenient grace to the sinner to give him an ability to believe the gospel. Prevenient grace enables the individual to accept God's gift of eternal life but does not ensure that he'll accept it. (Augustine also spoke of prevenient grace but believed it could not be resisted.)

Prevenient grace is important to understand because some Calvinists stereotype all Arminians as semi-Pelagian. Pelagius taught that people are born morally neutral and don't need God's grace. In contrast, Arminians say people are sinners by nature and absolutely do need God's grace in order to respond to the gospel.

God gives us choices to test us.

God said to Moses, "I will rain down bread from heaven for you. The people are to go out each day and gather enough for that day. In this way I will test them and see whether they will follow my instructions" (Exodus 16:4).

After the death of Joshua, the Lord said of the pagan nations around Israel, "I will use them to test Israel and see whether they will keep the way of the LORD and walk in it" (Judges 2:22).

King David said, "I know, my God, that you test the heart and are pleased with integrity" (1 Chronicles 29:17).

James promised, "Blessed is the man who perseveres under trial, because when he has stood the test, he will receive the crown of life that God has promised to those who love him" (James 1:12).

It's difficult to understand how God could say he tests us if he has predetermined exactly how we're going to respond.

If loving God really means something, then the choice to follow him must be both real and meaningful.

God is certainly capable of overruling me, and he's entitled to do so whenever he wishes. But if God predetermines every choice I make, then when I sin, he's causing me to do evil. Surely what prompts me to do evil are the forces at work within me, through my sin nature that dishonors God. If it were God who prompted me to sin, and sin is an act against God, then God would be acting against himself (see James 1:13–14).

Countless passages of Scripture would be nonsensical without at least a degree of free will. For instance, "No temptation has overtaken you that is not common to man. God is faithful, and he will not let you be tempted beyond your ability, but with the temptation he will also provide the way of escape, that you may be able to endure it" (1 Corinthians 10:13, ESV). Isn't the meaning of this verse that God allows us to face only the temptations we're capable of choosing to resist, by calling upon his power to do so? This affirms both God's sovereignty and our freedom to make the right choice. However, the provision that God will "provide the way of escape, that you may be able to endure it" doesn't seem to guarantee the end results, since it's clear that even God's children sometimes surrender to temptation. And when we do, we're held accountable.

Both Arminian and Calvinist pastors continuously call upon their people to make choices to follow Christ, reject false doctrine, and embrace the truth (including the truth about God's sovereignty). They also challenge unbelievers to place their faith in Christ. Surely we all believe in *some* degree of meaningful human choice, both for believers and unbelievers. God can and does move the hearts of people to draw them toward himself, but while he empowers them to choose to believe, it's also true that they genuinely choose to believe.

Whether Christ's invitation in Revelation 3:20 is understood to be made to unbelievers or believers, it surely portrays God as taking the initiative to extend an offer, and the human recipient of the offer being able to choose whether or not to open the door: "Behold, I stand at the door and knock. If anyone hears my voice and opens the door, I will come in to him and eat with him, and he with me" (Revelation 3:20, ESV).

A Calvinist may argue that the ability to open the door can only be granted by God, and whenever he does so, the person will indeed open the door. Most Arminians would say God must indeed grant the ability, but that he always does so, through prevenient grace—which the person, in an act of free will, may resist, choosing instead not to open the door.

The indwelling Holy Spirit endows us with new power to choose.
Regeneration changes our hearts, thereby changing the inclination of our wills. Once regenerated, we can choose a better way because, as new people in Christ, we *want* a better way (see 2 Corinthians 5:17), giving us greater freedom of choice than we had while in bondage to sin. "You, however, are controlled not by the sinful nature but by the Spirit, if the Spirit of God lives in you" (Romans 8:9).

Regeneration empowers the formerly blind to see and the formerly uncomprehending to understand the things of God (see 1 Corinthians 2:12–16; 2 Corinthians 4:4, 6; Colossians 3:10). Regeneration renews the will, enabling us to make godly choices (see Philippians 2:13; 2 Thessalonians 3:5). Once we're born again, sin is still present in our lives (see Romans 6:11–14; 1 John 1:8–2:2), but we have supernatural power to overcome sin, for we've died to sin (see Romans 6:6–9).

The fact that some believers do not live in this victory provided in Christ suggests a real ability to choose to accept or reject the Holy Spirit's empowerment.

Even limited choices can be meaningful and consequential.
A prisoner may choose to read, watch television, lift weights, write letters, pray, think about his family, or plot an escape. But he cannot visit a coffee shop downtown or catch a plane to London. The man in bondage makes meaningful choices—free, yet within very real confines.

> Our freedom to choose, though restricted, remains meaningful and consequential.

Years ago, Nanci and I had a fence put up to keep our grandsons away from the road. They freely make many choices. But knowing them, we realized it wasn't enough to say, "Don't go out on the street." For their sakes, we restricted their choices. The fence gives them real but limited choices within the yard.

Does God grant real, even if limited, freedom to us? Yes, we use it when we cook and paint and sing and laugh and play. He gives us the power to tell the truth or to lie.

Does a woman have a choice of where to go to college or to work or whom to marry, or whether or not to cheat on her taxes? Call it free will, meaningful choice, or anything else; it is God-given and real. If it isn't, then our decisions and our lives are merely illusions, and calling upon ourselves or others to make any choices at all would be senseless.

Real choices are nearly always open to us. Even when we lack strength to do some things, we can still do others.

We should be grateful for the freedom of choice granted us.

I began this chapter with the heroic choice Professor Liviu Librescu made to save the lives of his students on a day when an evildoer killed thirty-two people at Virginia Tech. I don't know whether the professor was a Christ-follower, but I do know that in the face of death, Librescu made a brave, meaningful, and consequential choice.

What made his choice both powerful and significant is that *he could have chosen differently*. But he made the right choice, and his students and their families remain deeply grateful that he did.

Notes

The second epigraph is from Charles Dickens, *A Christmas Carol* (London, William Heinmann, 1906), 21.

1. Alvin Plantinga, *God, Freedom, and Evil* (Grand Rapids, MI: Eerdmans, 1974), 30.

2. C. S. Lewis, *Mere Christianity,* in *The Complete C. S. Lewis Signature Classics* (New York: HarperOne, 2002), 47–48.

3. Lewis, *Mere Christianity,* in *Signature Classics,* 48.

4. C. S. Lewis, "The Efficacy of Prayer," in *The World's Last Night: And Other Essays* (Boston: Mariner Books, 2002), 9.

5. John Calvin, *Institutes,* 1.264, 266 (2.2.7–8), quoted in Wayne A. Grudem, *Systematic Theology: An Introduction to Biblical Doctrine* (Leicester, England: InterVarsity; Grand Rapids, MI: Zondervan, 1994), 330.

6. Calvin, *Institutes* 1:262 (2.2.6), quoted in Grudem, *Systematic Theology,* 330.

7. Charles G. Finney, *Lectures on Systematic Theology* (Fairfax, VA: Xulon, 2002), 1:62.

8. Roger Olson, *Arminian Theology: Myths and Realities* (Downers Grove, IL: InterVarsity, 2006), 63.

9. Olson, *Arminian Theology,* 63.

10. Martin Luther, Desiderius Erasmus, *Luther and Erasmus: Free Will and Salvation* (London: Westminster, 1969), 111.

11. Martin Luther, *The Bondage of the Will* (New York: Digireads.com Publishing, 2009), 65–66.

12. Olson, *Arminian Theology,* 116.

13. R. C. Sproul, "Augustine and Pelagius," Leadership U, www.leaderu.com /theology/augpelagius.html.

14. John Calvin, *The Bondage and Liberation of the Will: A Defense of the Orthodox Doctrine of Human Choice Against Pighius* (Grand Rapids, MI: Baker, 1996), 69.

15. Wayne Grudem, *Systematic Theology: An Introduction to Biblical Doctrine* (Grand Rapids, MI: Zondervan, 1994), 192–93.

16. Jacob Arminius, "Disputation 11: On the Free Will of Man and Its Powers," section 7, *Complete Works of Arminius,* www.ccel.org/ccel /arminius/works1.v.xii.html.

17. *Documents of the English Reformation 1526–1701,* ed. Gerald Lewis Bray (Cambridge, UK: James Clarke, 1994), 454.

18. Brian Abasciano and Martin Glynn, "An Outline of the FACTS of Arminianism vs. the TULIP of Calvinism," Society of Evangelical Arminians, February 28, 2013, http://evangelicalarminians.org /an-outline-of-the-facts-of-arminianism-vs-the-tulip-of-calvinism/.

19. Jonathan Edwards, *A Careful and Strict Inquiry,* Books for the Ages, AGES Software (Rio, WI: Master Christian Library Series, 2000), 10.

5

Main Views of Sovereignty and Choice

Our God is in heaven;
    he does whatever pleases him.

Psalm 115:3

You will certainly carry out God's purpose, however you act, but it makes a difference to you whether you serve like Judas or like John.

C. S. Lewis

While this book will not end the theological controversy surrounding the relationship between divine sovereignty and human freedom, this chapter should shed some light on various approaches to this issue.

People generally accept some variation of three central positions: libertarianism, determinism, and compatibilism (the latter is often referred to as "soft determinism"). Some add a fourth, Molinism, as its own self-contained system, but I believe it makes more sense when seen as a viewpoint that can be embraced within any of the other positions.

It's important to understand that in philosophy these terms are not distinctly Christian. Atheists can be determinists, libertarians, or compatibilists, though they utterly reject biblical authority.[1] In contrast, the terms Calvinist and Arminian are distinctly Christian. They refer historically to those who (1) believe the Bible and are either hard determinists or compatibilists (Calvinists) or (2) believe the Bible and are libertarians (Arminians). This is why to this point I've chosen mainly to use the terms Calvinist and Arminian. However, to explore the issues more clearly and deeply, we need to broaden our vocabulary.

Whether or not you use the terms libertarian, hard determinist, or compatibilist after reading this book, it's important to understand the underlying concepts. Once learned, the terminology will clarify rather than confuse. You'll gain insight by comparing these positions and deciding which of them you think Scripture most supports.

I recommend two books (each with multiple authors): *Four Views on Divine Providence* and *Predestination and Free Will*.[2] Both books present arguments by a proponent of each view, then each author critiques the others. This approach is invaluable, because it allows you to measure the responses against *actual* positions. If you have an open mind, at times you may find yourself buying into an author's position—you feel that, overall, his position makes sense. Then when you read the criticisms of that position from the other authors, you may change your opinion or at least modify it. In the end, you'll understand the strengths and weaknesses of each position as presented by intelligent people who hold them, and challenged by equally intelligent people who don't.

Learning involves respectfully listening to the viewpoints of others. So when you hear the different positions, try not to reject or refute them until you understand them.

"Let every person be quick to hear, slow to speak, slow to anger" (James 1:19, ESV).

Libertarianism means the freedom to make contrary choices.

Libertarianism claims that humans can choose between alternatives and that freedom and determinism cannot coexist. Most Arminians consider themselves libertarians.

Libertarian free will holds that we choose freely despite the inclinations of our human nature. If a choice is free and we choose option A, then we could instead have chosen B or any other option. Libertarians believe this freedom of contrary choice is vital to our humanity and essential for moral responsibility. Despite other influences, people's choices remain their own, without total "slavery to sin" or outside causes determining that they choose a certain way. Only if this is true, libertarians argue, can we be held responsible for our actions. (While many Calvinists believe in free will, they do not believe in libertarian free will; that is, they believe in a will that chooses freely according to its nature but that is not capable of choosing contrary to its nature.)

John Wesley said, "Were human liberty taken away, men would be as incapable of virtue as stones."[3]

Arminian theologian Jack Cottrell defines libertarianism this way:

> God has created us as persons with the innate power to initiate actions without interference, coercion, or fore-ordination. This does not imply total autonomy, since the will operates within the boundaries of God's controlling sovereignty and human finitude. It does include, however, the ability to choose between moral opposites, without the choice being fixed or determined (either ahead of time or at the time) by some power outside the person himself.[4]

Christian libertarians, also known as Arminians, view God's power as infinite but believe he has sovereignly chosen to delegate significant power of choice to his creatures, including humans, demons, and the devil. This is not a small-scale delegation, or it would not permit broad statements such as this: "The whole world lies in the power of the evil one" (1 John 5:19, ESV).

In terms of what actually happens on the fallen earth, libertarianism might look like this (I say "creatures'" choices here in order to include demons and Satan, not just humans):

Creatures' Choices   God's Choices

No Arminian would say God's sovereignty is equalized by creatures' choices, only that God has sovereignly delegated very significant power of choice to his creatures. Given that qualification, some Arminians might accept the above depiction, while others wouldn't.

A Calvinist, however, would reject this picture of libertarianism, citing Isaiah 40:15: "Surely the nations are like a drop in a bucket; they are regarded as dust on the scales." Believing that it undercuts God's sovereignty, they would likely see libertarianism as looking more like this:

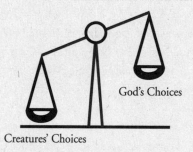

God's Choices

Creatures' Choices

An Arminian would reject this diagram for making man look more powerful than God. On the other hand, he might affirm the scales being more balanced, saying, "It was God's choice to grant free will, and he has put heavy weight on the choices of Satan, demons, and evil people." Paul says, "Our struggle is not against flesh and blood, but against the rulers, against the authorities, against the powers of this dark world and against the spiritual forces of evil in the heavenly realms" (Ephesians 6:12). God's sovereignty is compatible with his enemies exercising their God-given power.

Determinism means God's free choices are at work in his creatures' choices.

Determinism affirms that "acts of the will, occurrences in nature, or social or psychological phenomena are causally determined by preceding events or natural laws."[5] Believers would add that the causes include God's direct intervention, as well as the state of human nature and desires.

Calvinists are determinists, but to varying degrees. Most object to hard determinism, with its fatalism, often associated with hyper-Calvinism (more on that later). Compatibilists call themselves soft determinists, believing that determinism and responsible choice are compatible.[6]

Compatibilists believe God is free to overrule creatures' choices but is also free to choose not to, whenever he can accomplish his sovereign plan through their freely made choices, right or wrong. God is just as sovereign by determining to grant his creatures real choice as he would be by determining their every thought and action (as hard determinists believe he does).

Many Arminians believe that if determinism in any form is true, God-given freedom to choose—with a possible contrary choice—does not exist. They're incompatibilists in that they don't believe determinism is or can be compatible with free will. Most believe that free will is eventually swallowed up and rendered meaningless by the determinist view of sovereignty.

Determinists, whether hard or soft, maintain that their viewpoint alone upholds God's sovereignty. That's because determinists define sovereignty in terms of ultimate control of all events. Libertarians, however, believe God's sovereignty means he's not accountable to anyone, but is free to grant liberty to creatures however he chooses, and he chooses to grant them considerable power. God does what he wants, but not everything that happens is what God wants. (Compatibilists recognize that there are different "wills" of God,[7] including his moral will, which is often violated, and his decretive will, which is always accomplished.)

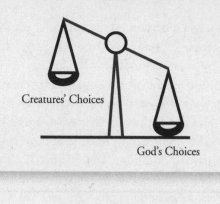

Hard Determinism

Creatures' Choices

God's Choices

Soft Determinism

Creatures' Choices

God's Choices

A hard determinist affirms that creature choices are directly predetermined by God. While the hard determinist says creatures are fully responsible for their choices, it's difficult to understand how or why. The creature's volition seems to have no substance, and therefore I depict in the scales diagram the weight of God's decisions being absolute and creatures' choices weighing nothing.

A soft determinist (or compatibilist) believes that God's choices far outweigh his creatures' choices, and that in the end, even evil choices are used by God for the fulfillment of his plan. He would agree that creature choices have *some* weight, yet they do not counterbalance God's choices in any significant way, and creature choices certainly do not thwart God's. So I've shown creature choices with some weight, but little in comparison to God's.

Compatibilism affirms that free will and determinism can coexist.

Compatibilism holds that free will (understood as people being able to make meaningful choices for which they're morally responsible) can coexist with determinism (understood as God remaining completely in control, never thwarted by his creatures' choices). Compatibilists believe that much that happens in this fallen world violates God's moral will, but everything that happens is in accord with his decretive will (defined as "the sovereign, efficacious will by which God brings to pass whatever He pleases by His divine decree"[8]).

How do the three main views handle all choices?

Libertarianism holds that creatures' free will involves making choices for which they're morally responsible. Libertarians believe that for any choice the creature makes, a different one could have been made (otherwise it would be no choice at all). Arminians believe that libertarianism can coexist with sovereignty, understood as God remaining completely autonomous, and that he is not thwarted from carrying out his plans, even though much that happens in this world is contrary to his will.

Some libertarians tend to view compatibilism as, at its core, hard determinism with a facelift. Others understand the difference between compatibilism and hard determinism, but they don't think compatibilism solves the problem of harmonizing sovereignty and human choice.

The following three diagrams portray the viewpoints differently. God's action is portrayed in the slanted lines that move upward toward the left, while man's action is shown by lines moving upward to the right. (These particular drawings were inspired by two in D. A. Carson's *Divine Sovereignty and Human Responsibility*. The explanations are my own.)

Libertarianism (Historic Arminianism)

Humans often act in contrary choice against God, who gives them freedom to do so.

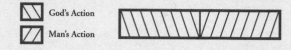

God's Action

Man's Action

With libertarianism, human actions are independent of God's actions. Though God can work sovereignly to set up certain circumstances, he doesn't interfere in actual creature choices.

This may sound as if Arminians, who are libertarians, would not believe in the doctrine of predestination. But they do. Arminius defined predestination like you might expect Calvin to have done: "The Election of men to Salvation, and the Reprobation of them to Destruction."[9]

However, the Arminian position sees God as predetermining the fates of all those who will believe and all those who will not, but not predetermining who will or will not believe. Jack Cottrell says, "God predestines believers to go to heaven, just as he predestines unbelievers to go to hell. But he does not predestine anyone to become and remain a believer, or to remain an unbeliever. This is a choice made by each individual, a choice that is foreknown by God."[10]

In *Classical Arminianism*, F. L. Forlines states, "Our gospel says that God has predestinated salvation for everyone who believes in Jesus Christ and He has predestinated that all who do not believe in Jesus Christ will be condemned to eternal death."[11]

There are secular hard determinists, but Bible-believing hard determinists have historically been called hyper-Calvinists. They believe that the real volition acting in all creatures' choices is that of God himself, not his creatures. Peter Toon points out that the terms *false Calvinism* and *high Calvinism* were used late in the eighteenth century in reference to the same doctrinal views that came to be called hyper-Calvinism in the nineteenth century.[12]

Hard Determinism (Hyper-Calvinism)

God directly determines all individual choices to accomplish his purposes.

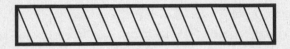

Sometimes the term hyper-Calvinist has been applied to five-point Calvinists or "anyone more Calvinistic than I am." This is a misuse of the term. Historically, hyper-Calvinism has been used of those teaching that God saves the elect through his sovereign will without human efforts to that end, such as evangelism, preaching, and prayer.

In regard to the sovereignty and free-will issue, the hyper-Calvinist label is sometimes used of those who see each and every human thought and action, good and evil, as completely dictated by God, so that human choice is effectively illusory and meaningless. This is depicted in the diagram above where every line is moving in the same direction: God is the only one whose choices matter and are therefore real.

Hard determinism flies in the face of the biblical passages cited in chapter 4. It would seem to make those passages a pretense, since people who appear to be choosing are really not, and people who appear to be offered a choice they could make are really not.

Hyper-Calvinism is Calvinism taken to an extreme, especially to the point of undermining evangelism and missions.

Hyper-Calvinism holds that since the elect must be saved and the non-elect cannot be saved, therefore evangelism and missions ultimately are pointless and ill-advised. A famous example of hyper-Calvinism occurred at a British ministers' gathering in 1787, when William Carey declared his desire to go to India as a missionary. One pastor responded, "Young man, sit down; when God pleases to convert the heathen, He will do so without your help or mine."[13]

Hyper-Calvinists—and though I seldom see this mentioned I think it's important—don't normally refer to themselves as such; they simply call themselves Calvinists. Mainstream Calvinism is not hyper-Calvinism, nor are five-point Calvinists or enthusiastic Calvinists or obnoxious Calvinists thereby hyper-Calvinists. (Hyper-Calvinists are often obnoxious, to be sure, but that's not what the term means.)

Of course, many people do reject true Calvinism. But the "Calvinism" some people reject is actually hyper-Calvinism. Just as mainstream Arminians shouldn't be written off as Pelagians, so mainstream Calvinists shouldn't be written off as hyper-Calvinists. Let's keep our focus on the actual theology—not personalities, past experiences, or stereotypes based on extremes.

Phil Johnson, a five-point Calvinist, states that he's "concerned about some subtle trends that seem to signal a rising tide of hyper-Calvinism, especially within the ranks of young Calvinists and the newly Reformed. I have seen these trends in numerous Reformed theological forums on the Internet, including mailing lists, Web sites, and Usenet forums."[14]

Johnson says this theology is characterized by "an imbalanced and unbiblical notion of divine sovereignty." He warns, "Virtually every revival of true Calvinism since the Puritan era has been hijacked, crippled, or ultimately killed by hyper-Calvinist influences."[15]

Compatibilism (Historic Calvinists)

Humans choose and sin freely, yet God maintains control and uses even sin to accomplish his purposes.

Compatibilists, as "soft determinists," do not go as far as hard determinists, or hyper-Calvinists, in that they emphatically affirm meaningful human choice with full human responsibility and accountability for our choices. But they go much further than libertarians, in that they say while God does permit and allow, he also ordains or decrees, which means more than "permit," but less than "create" or "cause."

Some Calvinists go further still, citing the King James Version translation of Isaiah 45:7, that has God say, "I...create evil." But the Hebrew word *ra* is used not only of moral evil but of the disastrous judgment of God upon moral evil. Hence the NIV translates *ra* in this verse as "disaster": "I form the light and create darkness, I bring prosperity and create disaster; I, the LORD, do all these things." Most translations render it as either "disaster" (as in GNT, HCSB) or "calamity" (ESV, NASB, NET, NKJV).

As in Isaiah 45:7, so in Jeremiah 11:17; 32:23; and Amos 3:6—God brings *ra,* disastrous consequences, to deal with people's *ra,* moral evil. God righteously brings terrible judgment upon human evil. We may feel that terrible judgment is itself evil, but in fact it is righteous. God brings disaster upon evil and can use evil when he so chooses, but he is in no sense the source of moral evil.

Calvin asked of the human fall into sin, "why, pray, should it be made a charge against the heavenly Judge, that he was not ignorant of what was to happen?... For as it belongs to his wisdom to foreknow all future events, so it belongs to his power to rule and govern them by his hand."[16] While God did not make humans sin, he did not surrender his governance over them.

Calvin firmly believed that God being sovereign did not mean he was to blame for human evil: "Therefore man's own wickedness corrupted the pure nature which he had received from God, and his ruin brought with it the destruction of all his posterity. Wherefore, let us in the corruption of human nature contemplate the evident cause of condemnation (a cause which comes more closely home to us), rather than inquire into a cause hidden and almost incomprehensible in the predestination of God."[17]

Compatibilism differs from hard determinism in that human choices are authentic and hence are distinct from God's choices. Compatibilism differs from libertarianism in that these human choices do not occur outside the realm of God's design, carried out by his governance that can bring good even out of evil. God is free to influence or overrule human choices however and whenever he wishes, for whatever purpose he wishes, so that the creature's capacity for contrary choice—whether or not it is regarded as normative—is not essential.

Compatibilism's biggest weakness—not as a system but as an inconsistency of some who hold it—may be its tendency to say that sovereignty and human choice are fully compatible, while proceeding to minimize human choice. Compatibilists are almost never in danger of sounding like libertarians, but at times they do sound like hard determinists.

Libertarians believe determinism, or at least universal determinism, is incompatible with human freedom.

Arminius wrote, "Because [God's] grace is interwoven with the nature of humanity in such a way as not to destroy the freedom of the will, but rather to give it proper direction and to correct its depravity, it allows the creature to devise actions of his own accord."[18]

This is an important distinction because Arminius believed it was *not* human merit but God's grace that enabled our choices. Still, this is quite different from any form of Calvinism, which believes God doesn't just enable the sinner to turn to God if his heart is so inclined, but actively gives him a new heart prior to conversion enabling his belief in God. Arminius affirmed total depravity yet said God's grace can "correct its depravity" in order to give his creature a free choice.

Cottrell argues, "All forms of determinism, which by definition deny the existence of truly free will, are inconsistent with the reality of sin. Without the ability to choose, one can neither be praised for good choices nor held responsible for wrong choices."[19]

William Lane Craig's dismissal of universal determinism is pointed:

> Universal, divine determinism makes reality into a farce. The whole world becomes a vain and empty spectacle. There are no free agents in rebellion against God, whom God seeks to win through his love, and no one who freely responds to that love

and freely gives his love and praise to God in return. The whole spectacle is a charade whose only real actor is God Himself. Far from glorifying God, [it] denigrates God.[20]

Craig, relentless in his critique of the total-control determinism he sees in the Calvinistic view of sovereignty, adds these comments: "A sort of vertigo sets in, for everything that you think, even this very thought itself, is outside your control. Determinism could be true; but it is very hard to see how it could ever be rationally affirmed, since its affirmation undermines the rationality of its affirmation."[21]

Cottrell also argues that God's sovereignty doesn't take the form of determinism: "Thus in the face of personal calamity and suffering it is probably improper to ask, 'Why is God doing this to me?' In all likelihood God himself is not doing it; it is probably the result of somebody's free-will choice either directly or indirectly."[22]

A compatibilist would say to Cottrell that just because a person or a demon chose to do something bad doesn't remove God's choices from the equation. After all, Joseph said to his brothers, "you meant evil against me, but God meant it for good" (Genesis 50:20, NIV 2011). And Paul "was given" by God the thorn in the flesh that was a harassing "messenger of Satan" (2 Corinthians 12:7).

This is why compatibilists aren't persuaded when it's pointed out that human or demonic choices are behind a life circumstance. Compatibilists believe God is above both the circumstances *and* the creatures who choose. He is capable of not only using their choices after the fact to accomplish his purposes, but of intending all along these life difficulties, which he'll sovereignly work together for his children's good (see Romans 8:28).

As determinism is difficult to reconcile with many creature-choice passages, libertarianism is difficult to reconcile with many sovereignty passages.

Some determinists, in my opinion, tend to give a token nod to human freedom without explaining how, if everything is predetermined, there can be any real creaturely freedom. Similarly, some libertarians tend to give a token nod to God's sovereignty, without explaining how God can elect or predestine people who have no substantial restraints on their freedom.

Consider these verses:

> The LORD foils the plans of the nations;
> he thwarts the purposes of the peoples.
> But the plans of the LORD stand firm forever,
> the purposes of his heart through all generations.
> (Psalm 33:10–11)

> The LORD works out everything for his own ends—
> even the wicked for a day of disaster. (Proverbs 16:4)

To the Calvinist, who believes in some form of determinism, these passages are definitive. The cumulative weight of such Scriptures indicates that God controls the events of human history as well as our daily lives. That idea should give us great comfort, especially when we recognize that "the LORD directs the steps of the godly. He delights in every detail of their lives" (Psalm 37:23, NLT).

> God is sovereign over the events of human history as well as our daily lives; that idea should give us great comfort.

On the other hand, the Arminian has his own definitive passages, as for instance, Jesus weeping over Jerusalem and saying, "How often would [Greek *thelo*] I have gathered your children together as a hen gathers her brood under her wings, and you would [*thelo*] not!" (Matthew 23:37, RSV). Jesus uses the same word for what *he* willed as for what *fallen creatures* willed. And whose will was realized? That of his fallen creatures. Jesus is mourning their choice to exercise their will against him.

Similarly, God tells the people of Israel it is within their power to make or not to make certain choices, good or bad: "Now what I am commanding you today is not too difficult for you or beyond your reach.... No, the word is very near you; it is in your mouth and in your heart so you may obey it" (Deuteronomy 30:11, 14).

Just as Calvinists insist a biblical view of sovereignty must recognize Psalm 33:10–11 and Proverbs 16:4, Arminians insist it must recognize Matthew 23:37 and Deuteronomy 30:11, 14. I believe both of them are absolutely right. It's not our job to pick and choose between Bible passages we like or don't like, but to believe all of them—even when it bursts the seams of our minds and we can't understand how to reconcile these verses (and hundreds of others).

Molinism attempts to meld free will with sovereignty.

Molinism was named after Luis de Molina (1535–1600), a priest who developed this viewpoint. It claims that people are free to choose, but using "middle knowledge," God has arranged the world knowing what will be freely chosen by everyone when placed in any particular circumstance. By arranging those circumstances to accomplish his sovereign ends, God foreknows the future and chooses accordingly, allowing him to accomplish his purpose as fully as if he'd predetermined every aspect.

"Middle knowledge" is the theory that God knows not only everything that *has* or *will* ever happen (the facts) but also knows exactly what *would* have happened, had things been different (the counter-factuals). A counter-factual is anything a person could have done but chose not to. Middle knowledge can be supported by a variety of passages (such as Jeremiah 38:17–18; Ezekiel 3:6–7; Matthew 12:7; 24:43; 1 Corinthians 2:8).

As the following diagram suggests, an exhaustive knowledge of counter-factuals, could-haves, and would-haves would provide God with an unlimited ability to carry out his sovereign plans in detail while allowing his creatures free choice.

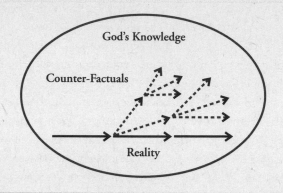

This means God knows *exactly* what would have happened if you'd chosen to work a different job, marry a different person, or gone or not gone to that Bible study or barbecue.

Molina believed in libertarian free will. Arminians who embrace middle knowledge call themselves Molinists, while some Calvinists who don't agree with libertarianism integrate the idea of middle knowledge into their compatibilist perspective, sometimes using the term Molinism and sometimes not.

Seeing middle knowledge and counter-factuals as a part of God's omniscience means God knows even more, far more, than all the facts of past, present, and future. He knows everything that ever could be if anything were different at any place and time in history. He can therefore exercise his sovereign power with exhaustive knowledge, affecting ultimate outcomes.

Molinists point to passages such as Christ's saying to Capernaum, "For if the mighty works done in you had been done in Sodom, it would have remained until this day" (Matthew 11:23, ESV) to show that God knows not only what did happen but also what would have happened. Furthermore, he knows not only what will happen, but also what would happen if other factors were in place.

Believing that Molinism explains God's providence and predestination, William Lane Craig, a leading advocate, calls it "one of the most fruitful theological ideas ever conceived."[23]

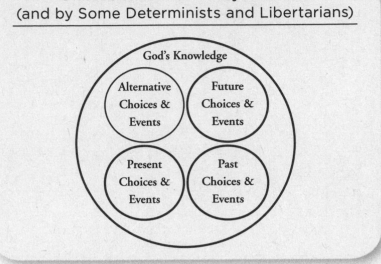

Omniscience Viewed by Molinists
(and by Some Determinists and Libertarians)

God's Knowledge

Alternative Choices & Events

Future Choices & Events

Present Choices & Events

Past Choices & Events

Calvinist Terence Tiessen writes, "With 'middle knowledge' God is able to...accomplish his plan without violating the responsible freedom he has given to his creatures."[24]

Molinism is more of a philosophical idea than a biblical doctrine, but various passages show that God knows how people would have chosen in other circumstances.

For example, Paul said, "None of the rulers of this age understood it, for if they had, they would not have crucified the Lord of glory" (1 Corinthians 2:8). Had God made Herod and Pilate understand certain truths, then Jesus wouldn't have been crucified. But his crucifixion was God's plan.

Like every viewpoint, Molinism has its weaknesses. Some critics of Molinism think it suggests God had to first learn the future choices of humans so he could plan accordingly. Others think God has always had all knowledge, which would mean he could plan as he wished, taking into account all choices that would ever be made under all possible circumstances.[25]

Here's an overview of the basic philosophical differences:

	Hard Determinism (Hyper-Calvinists)	Soft Determinism Compatibilism (Calvinists)	Libertarianism (Arminians)	Molinism (Calvinists or Arminians)
Sovereignty	God makes everything happen, good or evil, exactly as he has decided, to bring about his perfect plan, with all his creatures always doing exactly what he determines.	God works out his will and accomplishes his plan, doing good and permitting evil for which he has ultimate purposes; he grants people the ability to exercise meaningful choices, for which they are fully responsible.	God doesn't give an account to anyone. All he chooses to do happens. Everything angels and humans choose, he permits, including much he doesn't desire. He may or may not use for good all evils his children experience.	Knowing what humans will freely choose, and also what they would have chosen under different circumstances, God has created the world that would most glorify himself.
Evil	No matter how evil or how much suffering is involved, God is the ultimate (though not usually the immediate) cause of all evil and suffering, every detail of which is his will.	God accomplishes his decreed will while permitting violations of his moral will. God is not the source of evil, but can and does use evil to accomplish his ultimate plan.	Evil is a result of humans and demons choosing to rebel against God, but in the end God's plan will be victorious. (His purposes will prevail.)	Evil is caused by humans and demons working against God's will, but through setting in place certain circumstances, God is ultimately victorious.

Human Freedom	Human choices, good and evil, are predetermined by God through the person's internal makeup and external circumstances. Every choice is what God wills and decrees. People are not free to choose in any meaningful sense.	People make choices according to their nature and desires. They are fully responsible and accountable for their choices. Their choices are part of God's decretive will, yet those choices are real and meaningful.	While some choices are determined and all are limited, choices are free only when the person chooses an action they could have chosen not to do. There is real contrary choice. Some choices God wills; others are against God's will.	People choose freely, but God has arranged the world knowing what they will choose. For Arminians, God foreknows the future without ordaining it. For Calvinists, God ordains the future by the way he arranges it.
Sin	Human nature is pervaded by sin. Unbelievers are dead in sin and incapable of doing good. What appears to be human choice to repent of sin is actually God's choice on a person's behalf.	Human nature is pervaded by sin, leaving people incapable of choosing God's gift of salvation. They can make good choices but not saving choices. God's saving grace enables the elect and assures their repentance and belief in Christ.	Human nature is pervaded by sin, leaving people incapable of choosing Christ on their own. They can make good choices but not saving ones. God gives prevenient grace to all, enabling but not ensuring each person's choice to repent.	This varies by whether a particular Molinist is Calvinist or Arminian.

	Hard Determinism (Hyper-Calvinists)	Soft Determinism Compatibilism (Calvinists)	Libertarianism (Arminians)	Molinism (Calvinists or Arminians)
Salvation	Salvation is God's sovereign act for the elect, as is his reprobation to damnation for the non-elect. God accomplishes salvation without need of any human means. Evangelism and missions are unnecessary.	While making a genuine gospel offer to all, God chooses some and gives them power to become his children. Salvation is monergistic, the act of God alone, not requiring the cooperation of the unregenerate nature. God utilizes human instruments as message-bearers and persuaders.	The gospel is offered to all, and by God's prevenient grace, people are universally enabled to receive (but can still resist) God's invitation to be saved. While God does the work of salvation, the human cooperative response makes it synergistic. God utilizes human instruments.	God created this world knowing who would choose to believe in Christ. How this works out depends on whether a particular Molinist is Calvinist or Arminian.

Charles Spurgeon, a Calvinist, was opposed both by Arminians and hyper-Calvinists.

Though a five-point Calvinist, Spurgeon believed in free will, not the extensive free will of Arminianism or libertarianism, but more like what I'm calling meaningful choice. This alienated him from all hyper-Calvinists. Spurgeon was in a delicate position, being pastor of a church formerly pastored by John Gill, who said he must "utterly deny" the notion "that there are universal offers of grace and salvation made to all men."[26]

Spurgeon said, "During the pastorate of my venerated predecessor, Dr. Gill, this Church, instead of increasing, gradually decreased.... The system of theology with which many identify his name has chilled many churches to their very soul, for it has led them to omit the free invitations of the gospel, and to deny that it is the duty of sinners to believe in Jesus."[27]

Spurgeon said elsewhere,

Men sin as freely as birds fly in the air, and they are altogether responsible for their sin; and yet everything is ordained and foreseen of God. The foreordination of God in no degree interferes with the responsibility of man. I have often been asked by persons to reconcile the two truths. My only reply is—They need no reconciliation, for they never fell out. Why should I try to reconcile two friends? Prove to me that the two truths do not agree.... These two facts are parallel lines; I cannot make them unite but you cannot make them cross each other. Permit me also to add that I have long ago given up the idea of making all my beliefs into a system. I believe, but I cannot explain. I fall before the majesty of revelation, and adore the infinite Lord.[28]

Consider the zeal Spurgeon had for the hearts of people. In an 1858 sermon, based on Christ's words in Luke 14:23, "Compel them to come in," he refuted the hyper-Calvinist (hard determinist) position:

I should be destitute of all humanity if I should see a person about to poison himself, and did not dash away the cup; or if I saw another about to plunge from London Bridge, if I did not assist in preventing him from doing so; and I should be worse than a fiend if I did not now, with all love, and kindness, and earnestness, beseech you to "lay hold on eternal life."...

Some hyper-Calvinist would tell me I am wrong in so doing. I cannot help it. I must do it. As I must stand before my Judge at last, I feel that I shall not make full proof of my ministry unless I entreat with many tears that ye would be saved, that ye would look unto Jesus Christ and receive his glorious salvation.[29]

This sermon was widely criticized as sounding too Arminian. Spurgeon said to his critics, "My Master set His seal on that message. I never preached a sermon by which so many souls were won to God."[30]

In 1869 Spurgeon said to his congregation,

I am as firm a believer in the doctrines of grace as any man living, and a true Calvinist after the order of John Calvin himself; but if it be thought an evil thing to bid the sinner lay hold of eternal life, I will yet be more evil in this respect, and herein imitate my Lord and his apostles, who, though they taught that salvation is of grace, and grace alone, feared not to speak to men as rational beings and responsible agents.... Beloved friends, cling to the great truth of electing love and divine sovereignty, but let not these bind you in fetters when, in the power of the Holy Ghost, you become fishers of men.[31]

Spurgeon, one of the greatest Calvinist preachers of all time, served and preached in such a way as to put both Calvinists and Arminians in a difficult position. Calvinists must recognize that by passionately calling upon people to repent of their sins and choose Christ, Spurgeon sounded at times very much like John Wesley and other Arminian preachers.

On the other hand, Arminians are in an even more difficult position.

The five-point Calvinism they've heard described as "anti-evangelistic" and "lacking in compassion" was embraced by Spurgeon, who pleaded with sinners to follow Jesus and who founded and maintained sixty-five different institutions, including orphanages, social-welfare services, mission groups, and homes for unwed mothers.

Spurgeon, widely opposed by Arminians because of his staunch Calvinism, not only preached the gospel in church but his congregation took the gospel to the streets and homes of London more aggressively than any Arminian church of his time. He sent his church people door to door to distribute thousands of Bibles, Christian books, magazines, and tracts. In 1878 alone, his church's literature distributors made a total of 926,290 home visits.[32]

While hyper-Calvinism should be rejected on biblical grounds, many aspects of Calvinistic compatibilism fit with Scripture.

If some degree of divine determinism doesn't exist, at least in its softer form, how can God predestine his people according to his plan and work out "everything in conformity with the purpose of his will," as Ephesians 1:11 tells us? And what would Romans 9:16 mean: "So then it does not depend on the man who wills or the man who runs, but on God who has mercy" (NASB)?

As we saw in chapter 3, many Scriptures declare God's absolute sovereignty. He not only determines the times and boundaries of nations (see Acts 17:26) but also takes credit for natural processes (see Matthew 6:26, 30).

Arrogant Assyria viewed itself as controlling its own destiny, but God said, "Does the ax raise itself above him who swings it, or the saw boast against him who uses it?" (Isaiah 10:15). Hard determinists cite this passage to prove that humans are but instruments in God's hands. However, a human is not passive like an ax. People can exercise their own wills *and* be used by God to accomplish his.

A libertarian might object, "These passages may prove that God fully determines *some* things, but many passages suggest he leaves some choices up to humans." That may be true, but if so it undermines the purest forms of libertarianism which insist that human beings must *always* have the freedom of contrary choice. Hence, any libertarianism held to by Christians must be a qualified and nuanced libertarianism that still leaves a place for God's determinism. In other words, to be true to God's Word, Arminians should affirm meaningful divine sovereignty and providence, just as Calvinists should affirm meaningful and consequential human choice.

> People can exercise their own wills *and* be used by God to accomplish his.

God commands people to be holy and to keep his decrees (see Leviticus 20:7–8). But immediately after this command, God says, "I am the LORD, who makes you holy" (verse 8). Here we're told *it is God who makes us become what he commands us to be.* This is one of countless passages that inclines me toward compatibilism, even though I see that, like every position, it has its weaknesses. What seems clear in Scripture is that we choose and are accountable for our choices—yet God reigns over all, over everything he approves and disapproves of, including our choices. His Hand is over us, yet our hand is in his.

Because God wills things in two different senses, God's will is not always done, yet his will is never frustrated.

Some people who emphasize God's reign have told me, "God's will cannot be thwarted." If by "God's will" they mean his ultimate, decreed purpose, then yes, Ephesians 1:11 and other passages support this.

But if they mean that God's moral laws and stated desires cannot be violated, they're mistaken. Indeed, every single sin violates God's moral will. The prayer "Thy will be done in earth, as it is in heaven" (Matthew 6:10, KJV) assumes that God's will often is *not* currently done on earth.

Scripture says the omnipotent God desires many things that don't happen; for instance, he "desires all people to be saved and to come to the knowledge of the truth" (1 Timothy 2:4, ESV). Taking these words at face value, one would conclude that God's desire will not be fulfilled, since not all people will be saved (see Matthew 25:46).

> God's ultimate will stands firm even though his moral will is often violated.

As we've seen, Jesus wept over Jerusalem when he wanted one thing and Jerusalem wanted another (see Matthew 23:37). Yet Jesus didn't get what he said he wanted, while Jerusalem did, effectively resisting his will (to its own ruin).

Imagine a theologian saying, "God's will is sometimes A, when man's will is B. In some cases, man's will prevails instead of God's." This sounds like utter heresy to someone who believes in God's sovereignty. But we are still left with Matthew 23:37 about Jesus willing to gather the people of Jerusalem under his wings, but them willing otherwise. True, we need to place this passage alongside passages that emphatically declare God's sovereignty. But we should not act as if those passages neutralize this one. We should not put some passages over or under others—unless one passage is unclear and the others clear—but should instead affirm the truth of all. Too often we negate or undermine the meaning of one passage by too quickly calling upon another, not allowing the less popular passage to say what it says.

In the Matthew 23 passage, Jesus could certainly have overpowered the will of Jerusalem's people and forced them to submit to his will to minister to them. But he sovereignly chose not to do so. One day Jesus will reign over the New Jerusalem, filled with people who willingly bow to his lordship. Ironically, Jerusalem's immediate *rejection* of his will was necessary to accomplish the ultimate *fulfillment* of his will.

The following diagram depicts one way of looking at the various aspects of God's will. His directive or moral will is what he tells us to do. His permissive will allows us to sin, violating his will—even moving the opposite direction. Yet our choice to rebel does not hamper the forward movement of God's overruling will, which reflects his sovereign plan in and over all things.

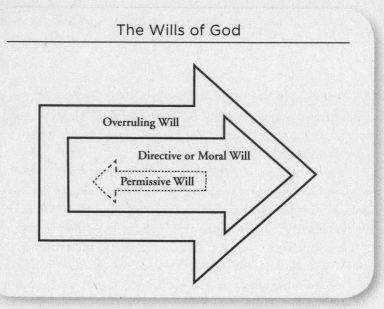

The Wills of God

Overruling Will

Directive or Moral Will

Permissive Will

Humans can and do reject and resist God: "You stiff-necked people, with uncircumcised hearts and ears! You are just like your fathers: You always resist the Holy Spirit!" (Acts 7:51).

If someone asked, "Can humans reject God's purposes for us?" how would you answer? My intuitive answer is no. Yet the Bible, without qualification, claims the Pharisees and experts in the law "rejected the purpose of God for themselves" (Luke 7:30, ESV). As a compatibilist, I can interpret this verse within my system, but I should understand why a libertarian will feel it fits his system better than mine.

While our views change, God does not.

Emotions run high on this issue and not simply because of the ongoing controversy. I'll never forget the horror I felt as a young Christian reading passages speaking of election and predestination. And yet today, ironically, many of the same passages that once troubled me I now consider my greatest source of comfort. God's sovereign grace is precious to me, as I know it is to many who see things somewhat differently than I do.

Thankfully, we can choose to say, together, "Some trust in chariots and some in horses, but we trust in the name of the LORD our God" (Psalm 20:7).

Notes

The second epigraph is from C. S. Lewis, *The Problem of Pain,* in *The Complete C. S. Lewis Signature Classics* (New York: HarperCollins, 2002), 616.

1. "Determinism and Free Will," *The Atheist Scholar* (blog), http://atheist scholar.org/Determinism.aspx.

2. Paul Kjoss Helseth et al., *Four Views on Divine Providence* (Grand Rapids, MI: Zondervan, 2011) and John Feinberg et al., *Predestination and Free Will: Four Views of Divine Sovereignty and Human Freedom,* (Downers Grove, IL: InterVarsity, 1986).

3. John Wesley, "On Divine Providence" (sermon 67), *Sermons on Several Occasions,* www.ccel.org/ccel/wesley/sermons.vi.xiv.html.

4. Jack Cottrell, *The Faith Once for All: Bible Doctrine for Today* (Joplin, MO: College Press Publishing, 2002), 157.

5. *Merriam-Webster Online Dictionary,* s.v. "determinism," www.merriam -webster.com/dictionary/determinism.

6. A good presentation of compatibilism is D. A. Carson's *Divine Sovereignty and Human Responsibility: Biblical Perspective in Tension* (Eugene, OR: Wipf and Stock, 2002).

7. John Piper, "Are There Two Wills in God? Divine Election and God's Desire for All to Be Saved," Desiring God, January 1, 1995, www.desiringgod.org/articles/are-there-two-wills-in-god.

8. R. C. Sproul, "Comprehending the Decretive Will of God," Ligonier Ministries, www.ligonier.org/learn/devotionals/comprehending-decretive -will-god/.

9. Jacobus Arminius, *The Works of James Arminius, D.D.*, trans. James Nichols (Auburn, NY: Derby, Miller and Orton, 1853), 211.

10. Cottrell, *Faith Once for All*, 392.

11. F. L. Forlines, *Classical Arminianism: A Theology of Salvation*, ed. J. M. Pinson (Nashville: Randall House, 2011), 174.

12. Peter Toon, *The Emergence of Hyper-Calvinism in English Nonconformity, 1689–1765* (Eugene, OR: Wipf and Stock, 2011), n. p.

13. Michael N. Ivey, *A Welsh Succession of Primitive Baptist Faith and Practice*, transcribed on *The Reformed Reader*, www.reformedreader.org /history/ivey/ch06.htm.

14. Johnson, "A Primer on Hyper-Calvinism," www.spurgeon.org/~phil /articles/hypercal.htm.

15. Johnson, "A Primer on Hyper-Calvinism."

16. John Calvin, Henry Beveridge, trans., *Institutes of the Christian Religion*, Book III, Chap. XXI (Grand Rapids, MI: Eerdmans Publishing, 1997), 232.

17. Calvin, *Institutes*, 233.

18. W. Stephen Gunter, *Arminius and His "Declaration of Sentiments"* (Waco, TX: Baylor University Press, 2012), 118.

19. Cottrell, *Faith Once for All*, 169.

20. William Lane Craig, *A Reasonable Response: Answers to Tough Questions on God, Christianity and the Bible* (Chicago: Moody Publishers, 2013), 178.

21. Craig, *A Reasonable Response*, 177.

22. Cottrell, *Faith Once for All*, 222.

23. William Lane Craig, quoted in Greg Baxter, "God's Sovereignty and Human Freedom—Balanced Truth," *Baptist Bible Tribune*, www .tribune.org/?p=2283.

24. Terrance Tiessen, *Providence and Prayer: How Does God Work in the World?* (Downers Grove, IL: InterVarsity, 2000), 289–90.

25. For this and three other paragraphs in this section I am indebted to my research assistant Julia Stager; she wrote them, I revised.

26. John Gill, *The Doctrine of Predestination Stated, and Set in the Scripture Light* (Sermons and Tracts 1814–1815), III, 118, quoted in *The Life and*

Thought of John Gill (1697–1771): A Tercentennial Appreciation, ed. Michael A. G. Haykin (Leiden, The Netherlands: Brill, 1997), 28.

27. C. H. Spurgeon, *The Autobiography of Charles H. Spurgeon,* 1834–1854, comp. Susannah Spurgeon and Joseph Harrald (Chicago: Fleming H. Revell, 1898), 1:310.

28. C. H. Spurgeon, *Spurgeon's Sermons on Christmas and Easter* (Grand Rapids, MI: Kregel, 1995), 126.

29. C. H. Spurgeon, "Compel Them to Come In" (sermon 227, Royal Surrey Gardens, December 5, 1858), www.spurgeon.org/sermons/0227.htm.

30. C. H. Spurgeon, *Flashes of Thought: Being One Thousand Choice Extracts from the Works of C. H. Spurgeon* (London: Passmore and Alabaster, 1874), 182.

31. Spurgeon, *Flashes of Thought,* 182.

32. Spurgeon, *Autobiography,* 3:166.

Does Open Theism Resolve the Sovereignty/ Choice Paradox?

You know what I am going to say
even before I say it, LORD.

Psalm 139:4, NLT

[God] knows instantly and with a fullness of perfection that includes every possible item of knowledge
concerning everything that exists or could have
existed anywhere in the universe at any time in the
past or that may exist in the centuries or ages yet
unborn.

A. W. Tozer

At age ten, our daughter Karina sat behind me, next to her friend
Andrea, in a small plane that had to make a dramatic emergency
landing in Alaska. When our single engine failed, Barry Arnold, the missionary pilot, landed by a river at the base of two mountains. After our
rescue, Karina told me, "God must have a purpose for my life."

Six years later, a van full of high schoolers including Karina, coming home from a summer outreach, rolled over on a highway, yet caused only bumps and bruises. She told me, "This is the second time God spared my life. He must have a purpose."

When our daughter Angela was a teenager, doctors removed a large tumor from her body. As we awaited the test results in her hospital room, I received a call saying the son of our close friends, a missionary couple, had been in a terrible accident. A few hours later, Jonathan died. Angie's tumor was benign. God spared her life. Why didn't he spare Jonathan's?

We don't know. And it's precisely this human inability to know that spawns attempts at addressing the problem of God's sovereignty, human free will, and the existence of evil. One of these attempts is called *open theism*. Evaluating this worldview will allow us to further explore the main issues addressed differently by the other worldviews.

Does God's foreknowledge cause future events?

Proponents of open theism believe that God doesn't know in advance the future choices his free creatures will make. If he did, say open theists, then (1) there would be no such thing as free will, and (2) God, because he loves us, would not permit terrible evils to befall his children.

Let's take a closer look at both claims.

Clark Pinnock, a proponent of open theism, stated, "If God now knows that tomorrow you will select A and not B, then your belief that you will be making a genuine choice is mistaken."[1] Open theists claim that human freedom and divine foreknowledge of our choices are mutually exclusive. If God knows you'll drink a mocha at 3:09 p.m. tomorrow, then you're not free to abstain from drinking it. (Though *foreknowledge* sometimes has a deeper theological meaning, I here refer to it as God's prescience; that is, his simple knowledge of an event before it occurs.)

God knew in advance of Satan's fall and Adam and Eve's sin, but he did not cause it, for God does not tempt people to evil (see James 1:13). Yes, he could have kept them from sinning, and yes, he's accomplishing an ultimate plan of redemption. But foreknowledge and causation are not synonymous.

Suppose I travel to the future (something I rarely do) and see a certain quarterback throw a winning touchdown pass. Then I return to my time. Would my future knowledge rob him of his free choice to throw that pass? No.

Of course, unlike a human time traveler, God is fully capable of causing the quarterback to throw the pass and the receiver to catch it—but my point is, God's knowing what will happen does not *require* that he cause it to happen. Our freedom to choose is not inherently incompatible with God knowing our choices in advance.

> Open theists claim that human freedom and divine foreknowledge of our choices are mutually exclusive.

God sees the future with fixed certainty. That's why the Bible calls Jesus the Lamb slain from before the foundation of the world, not merely the Lamb who God *felt confident* would be slain.[2]

Does God change his mind and grow in understanding?

Open theists often cite 1 Samuel 15:11 to prove that God learns and changes his mind. God says, "I regret that I have made Saul king" (ESV). The word translated "I regret" is also rendered "I am grieved" (NIV). Again, in verse 35, "And the LORD regretted that he had made Saul king over Israel" (ESV).

Open theists argue that when God says he "regrets" something, he implies that he didn't know what would happen. He acted on the best knowledge he had at the time, but the bottom line is, God made a mistake.

Throughout history, Christians have understood that in 1 Samuel 15 (and similar passages), God accommodates his language to us, saying he "regrets" making Saul king to communicate powerfully that he grieves over sin. God is *not* saying, "If only I'd known back then..."

"He is not a man, that he should have regret" (verse 29, ESV). Here we find an unequivocal clarification in the immediate context, using the same Hebrew word from verses 11 and 35, warning us *not* to conclude *exactly* what open theists conclude—namely, that God regrets in the same way humans do.

> The God of the Bible is not undergoing a process of education; we change, he doesn't.

We can trust God's promises because he says, "I the LORD do not change" (Malachi 3:6). He's a God "who does not change like shifting shadows" (James 1:17).

If God learned things only when they happen, he would be learning every moment billions of pieces of new information. But the God of the Bible is not undergoing a constant process of education. He responds to his creatures, and he has and shows emotions (see Genesis 6:6; Exodus 32:10; Deuteronomy 1:37; Judges 2:18; 1 Kings 3:10; Psalm 103:13; Zephaniah 3:17; Ephesians 4:30). In that sense, God changes in his attitudes and actions in response to our repentance, prayers, or sin. But God doesn't change in his essence, character, knowledge, plans, or purposes. In those respects, we change; he doesn't.

God warns us, "You thought I was altogether like you. But I will rebuke you and accuse you to your face" (Psalm 50:21). He forbids innovative theologies that revise his attributes to fit our thinking.

I agree with Bruce Ware, who argued that God never regrets in the strong and ultimate sense, but in a weaker and more immediate sense.[3] He's not uncaring (he does regret), but he remains unchanging (he does not regret).

So how do we explain passages such as God promising judgment on Nineveh (see Jonah 3:4), then deciding to withhold judgment when the Ninevites repent (verse 10)? Wayne Grudem wrote, "These instances should all be understood as true expressions of God's *present* attitude or intention *with respect to the situation as it exists at that moment*. If the situation changes, then of course God's attitude or expression of intention will also change."[4]

Such change does not indicate inconsistency. God remains true to his unchanging nature by responding to repentance differently than he responds to evil: "If at any time I declare concerning a nation or a kingdom, that I will pluck up and break down and destroy it, and if that nation...turns from its evil, I will relent of the disaster that I intended to do to it" (Jeremiah 18:7–8, ESV).

Does God ever send suffering?

Another proponent of open theism, Gregory Boyd, wrote, "The open view, I submit, allows us to say consistently in unequivocal terms that the ultimate source of all evil is found in the will of free agents rather than in God."[5] Since Boyd includes suffering in "all evil," he believes God never sends us suffering.

Open theists suggest that had God known the horrible things that would occur—the rapes and killings and abuse—he might never have created this world as he did. Hence, God cannot be held responsible for his creatures' evil, since he couldn't foresee it.

Boyd describes how his father once asked him how a good God could allow Adolf Hitler to be born if he foreknew he would massacre millions. Boyd wrote, "The only response I could offer then, and the only response I continue to offer now, is that this was not foreknown as a certainty at the time God created Hitler."[6] While God can know in advance what *he* has planned to do, open theists claim he cannot know what his free *creatures* will choose to do. They believe this distances God from evil human choices and suffering. "The future is really open," wrote Clark Pinnock, "and not available to exhaustive foreknowledge *even on the part of God*" (italics mine).[7]

Open theism could be depicted like this when compared with the classic orthodox understanding of God's omniscience:

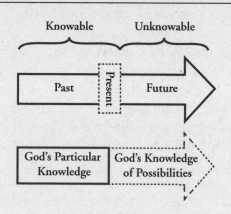

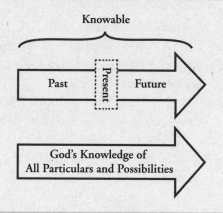

In contrast, historical orthodox Christianity in all its forms has believed that God knows the future as he knows the past and the present: exhaustively. This is what *omniscience* always meant.

Though open theists speak of God's omniscience, it's misleading for them to insist on using the term while departing from its historical meaning.

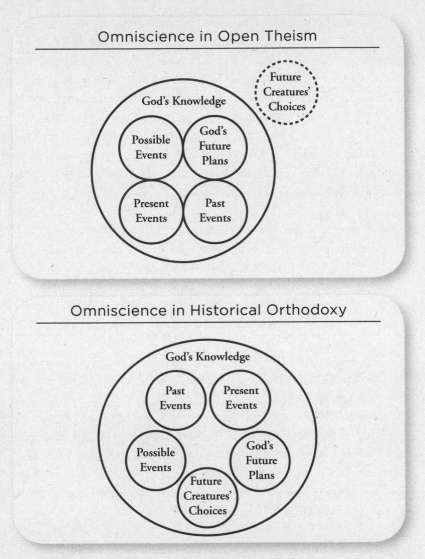

God knows all past, present, and future realities of every kind. He knows his creatures' choices as well as his own. Those who affirm "middle knowledge" add that God knows all possibilities, contingencies, and counter-factuals—not only everything that is or will be, but everything that would have been or could have been but isn't.

Can a partially unaware God bring greater comfort?

In *Is God to Blame?* Boyd called the traditional definition of God's omniscience misguided.[8] He tells the heartbreaking story of Melanie, who came to him for pastoral counsel, wondering why God had taken her only child, who at birth was strangled on her umbilical cord. Boyd wrote, "I asked, 'Does that seem like something a loving God would do? Can you picture Jesus doing that to someone?' Melanie was completely stunned by my reply.... I felt such grief for the tormented state her theology had put her in."[9] Boyd told Melanie that God didn't know in advance that her baby would die. He explained,

> We have no reason to assume God put Melanie and her husband
> through this tragic ordeal. Rather, we have every reason to assume
> God was and is at work to *deliver* Melanie and her husband from
> their ordeal....
>   It is most biblical and most helpful not to see God involved
> in the evils in this world but to interpret it in some other fashion.[10]

The key to Melanie's spiritual health, Boyd believes, lay in accepting that her child's death remained beyond God's knowledge and was not part of his plan.

If Boyd is right and God has no knowledge of future choices and events, then God wouldn't know the baby was going to suffocate until it actually began to die. But how does that solve the problem? Once God knew, why didn't he intervene? Or worse, since he could see everything leading up to the tragedy, he could have alerted the baby's doctors to the problem beforehand. But he didn't.

Does limited knowledge showcase God's unlimited power?

Boyd tells of Suzanne, who asked God to provide a husband with whom she could serve on the mission field. She met a man at college and sensed God's leading to marry him. Tragically, he turned out to be an unrepentant adulterer and left her and their child. Boyd said this about Suzanne's bitterness toward God:

I suggested to her that God felt as much regret over the confirmation he had given Suzanne as he did about his decision to make Saul king of Israel.... Not that it was a bad decision—at the time her ex-husband was a good man with a godly character. The prospects that he and Suzanne would have a happy marriage and fruitful ministry were, at the time, very good. Indeed, I strongly suspect that he had influenced Suzanne and her ex-husband toward this college with their marriage in mind.

The woman said she found comfort in Boyd's viewpoint. He concluded,

By framing the ordeal within the context of an open future, Suzanne was able to understand the tragedy of her life in a new way. She didn't have to abandon all confidence in her ability to hear God and didn't have to accept that somehow God intended this ordeal "for her own good." Her faith in God's character and her love toward God were eventually restored and she was finally able to move on with her life.[11]

But why should it help Suzanne to believe that she could again sense God's leading? After all, God might have another well-meaning prediction of a happy future, only to be proven wrong yet again. Shouldn't she rather think, *God already led me into a terrible marriage; who's to say he won't lead me somewhere worse next time?*

> There's a difference between *immediate* good and *ultimate* good. Accepting that difference requires faith.

Since open theists agree that God has total knowledge of every past event as well as complete knowledge of all current thoughts, surely he could see that this man's descent into adultery didn't "just happen." Why didn't God give Suzanne any hint of the truth beforehand?

Boyd also dismissed as naive the notion "that somehow God intended this ordeal 'for her own good.'" But is it really cruel of God to permit evil and intend it for our ultimate good as part of his plan, as Romans 8:28 says? True, there's a difference between *immediate* good and *ultimate* good. Accepting that difference requires faith.

Open theists suggest that the God of orthodoxy is distant and insensitive, while their God of openness is engaged, flexible, and loving. In fact, the God of historic, orthodox Christianity is a God who cares deeply about us, but who also has a purpose and plan even for the bad things we encounter. Open theism tries to persuade us we can love God more because he doesn't have a purpose in our suffering. Such a God may *seem* more lovable, but at what expense?

Where's the logic?
While some individuals like the way open theism addresses the sovereignty and free-will issues, and say they find comfort in open theism, I honestly see no logical basis for their comfort.

> The gospel of grace was not God's plan B.

Compare Melanie's and Suzanne's situations from two perspectives. In the traditional view, God knew from eternity past what would happen, and allowed it or ordained it (either theological perspective works) with a good ultimate purpose informed by his foreknowledge. In the open view, God didn't know in advance but only at the time the events unfolded. He had the power to stop them but chose not to. He had no purpose and plan in what happened.

What, exactly, is there to feel better about in the open view? That God has known of the evil and suffering a shorter time? In addition to contradicting Scripture, this viewpoint seemingly gives us much more to feel worse about.

We might compare the God of the Bible to a gifted surgeon who has carefully studied a patient's case and planned a specific procedure to accomplish a particular purpose. The God of open theism appears more like an emergency-room physician, just as skilled as others, but who doesn't know his patient's condition until the patient comes in the door. Therefore the physician must improvise, sometimes more successfully than others.

While open theists affirm most of the classic attributes of God, his lack of complete knowledge of future events is seen by them as an explanation for why he permits evil that they think a loving God would not permit if he knew in advance what was going to happen.

Such a viewpoint is utterly foreign to Scripture. God created the world fully knowing that sin would enter it, and fully knowing his redemptive response. The gospel of grace was not God's plan B; with sovereign knowledge, wisdom, and power. It was God's plan A from the beginning.

Scripture's response is that God's knowledge has no boundaries.

Open theism stands in contrast to the biblical and historical teaching that God knows absolutely everything. God is "perfect in knowledge" (Job 37:16). He "knows everything" (1 John 3:20).

"Your Father knows what you need before you ask him," and "even the very hairs of your head are all numbered" (Matthew 6:8; 10:30).

"Yes," an open theist will say, "but while God knows everything that *can* be known, future choices of his free creatures *can't* be known; at best they can be predicted without certainty."

But consider what David wrote: "O LORD, you have searched me and known me! You know when I sit down and when I rise up; you discern my thoughts from afar.... Even before a word is on my tongue, lo, O LORD, you know it altogether" (Psalm 139:1–2, 4, ESV). From eternity past, God knew everything that will happen on every day of our lives: "In your book were written, every one of them, the days that were formed for me, when as yet there was none of them" (verse 16, ESV).

When David asked God questions about the future, God gave him detailed answers about what Saul and the men of Keilah would do (see 1 Samuel 23:11–12). God knew their specific choices in advance.

God knows not only what choices his creatures will make, but also what would have happened (middle knowledge) if his creatures made different choices. To Chorazin and Bethsaida, Jesus stated, "If the miracles that were performed in you had been performed in Tyre and Sidon, they *would have repented* long ago" (Matthew 11:21).

Christians throughout church history, including both Arminian and Calvinist theologians, have believed that omniscience encompasses *all* knowledge. A. H. Strong described it as "God's perfect and eternal knowledge of all things…whether they be actual or possible, past, present, or future."[12] Bruce Ware pointed out, "The open view has not been advocated by any portion or branch of the Orthodox, Roman Catholic, or Protestant church throughout history."[13]

If God cannot know what will result from human and demonic choices, then given the vast number of free beings and the innumerable daily choices they make, God cannot know with certainty untold trillions of choices and subsequent events. Open theism contradicts both the Calvinist perspective of God's elective or causative foreknowledge *and* the Arminian perspective of his simple or noncausative foreknowledge.

I don't enjoy opposing a doctrine that seems to comfort suffering brothers and sisters. But I've included this chapter because I feel compelled to explain why I reject it. The classic Calvinist and Arminian viewpoints on sovereignty and free will both fall within the realm of biblical orthodoxy, though each emphasizes different parts. However, open theism redefines God himself, altering one of his most basic attributes, omniscience, in a misguided and unsuccessful attempt to make it more compatible with his love. This is why I consider open theism not to be an orthodox position.

God knows the end from the beginning.

Demons and false prophets may be able to guess certain aspects of the future, but they err on some points because finite beings can't know everything about the future.

In contrast, the Creator said, "I am God, and there is none like me. I make known the end from the beginning, from ancient times, what is still to come. I say: My purpose will stand, and I will do all that I please" (Isaiah 46:9–10). God can make known the end from the beginning only because he *knows* the end from the beginning. Nothing can surprise him or derail his plans.

God prophesied that Judas would betray Jesus for thirty pieces of silver and throw the money back to the priests (see Zechariah 11:13; compare Matthew 27:3–7).

Christ knew that a rooster at a specific place would crow at a specific time, after Peter would deny him *three* (not two or four) times (see Matthew 26:34, 69–75). Earlier, Jesus had said, "Simon, Simon, behold, Satan demanded to have you, that he might sift you like wheat, but I have prayed for you that your faith may not fail. And *when* you have turned again, strengthen your brothers" (Luke 22:31–32, ESV).

If Jesus knew the details of Peter's future choices—both that Peter would turn away from him and later turn back—why wouldn't he know the details about all *our* future choices?

God doesn't merely predict the future to a high degree of probability; he absolutely knows it in advance.

Boyd appears to claim that the future cannot be known because it doesn't exist. Refuting this seems to require only a single biblical proof of a time when God knows the future choices people will make. Since it's clear he knew Peter's future choices, then the future must be real in God's mind, disproving a major foundation of open theism.

Some argue that Jesus knew Peter well enough to accurately predict what he would do. But if divine prophecies involving human free choices can never be certain, then was Christ merely making lucky guesses?

Might Peter have chosen differently—say, denied Christ just twice—and Christ have been proven wrong? If so, what else might Christ have been wrong about?

But those who believe in a God who knows "the end from the beginning" (Isaiah 46:10) can find comfort that even though *they* don't know what lies ahead, their sovereign God does.

Ironically, Greg Boyd claims the God of open theism "can and does at times unilaterally intervene and work in a coercive way to bring about a certain state of affairs."[14] Doesn't this admission undermine both the claims and attractiveness of open theism?

Once God is recognized as *sometimes* violating self-determining human freedom, open theism's adamant case against both determinism and compatibilism seems nonsensical. After all, if he sometimes miraculously intervenes—even to the point of violating creaturely free will in acts of love and protection of his children—why in so many other cases does he not do so? Instead of God never being to blame for evil and suffering, doesn't this suggest he's *always* to blame?

In the situations of Melanie and Suzanne, whose heart-tugging stories capture the attractiveness of open theism, they should have been told that God *could have* and in fact sometimes *does* sovereignly intervene to change events, but in their cases, he did not. If God's love for his children is at stake, as Boyd clearly maintains, then doesn't that mean God didn't love Melanie and Suzanne enough to overrule their circumstances?

Open theism therefore not only takes away the assurance of Romans 8:28 that God will sovereignly work all things together for our good; it also fails to deliver its claim of God loving us all so much that, if only he could know in advance and stop evil from happening to us, he would always do so. In my opinion, promising the best of all worlds, open theism delivers the worst.

Paul Kjoss Helseth said it well: "While openness theologians would have us believe that they have a viable solution to the problem of evil in *general,* in fact they can only hope that those who have been traumatized by *particular* evils do not find out that their suffering could have been prevented if God had simply been inclined to act in their cases as he does from time to time in others, namely, coercively."[15]

God doesn't need to be rescued.

I don't believe in picking fights about secondary doctrinal issues. But I'm convinced there's a great deal at stake in open theism. God doesn't need us to rescue him from the problem of evil, particularly at such great cost.

Justin Taylor wrote, "Open theism is not just another intramural squabble among evangelicals. It is not a debate about second-order doctrines, minutiae, or peripheral matters. Rather, it is a debate about God and the central features of the Christian faith."[16]

I've noticed a domino effect in books that promote open theism. When someone diminishes or topples one of God's attributes, other attributes inevitably start to fall. In the cases of Melanie and Suzanne, God's lack of knowledge produced a lack of power to lovingly protect them. Once we begin to dismantle God's attributes, he ceases to be the only true God revealed in Scripture.

In 1981, the year my mother died of cancer, I read Rabbi Harold Kushner's best-selling book *When Bad Things Happen to Good People*. He desperately wanted to understand how God could have allowed a tragedy in his family. His answer came down to this: God wanted to do something about it, but unfortunately, he simply lacked the power. It was a sad book to read, but the thought never occurred to me that some evangelical pastors would one day be making similar arguments.

But that's what has happened with open theism. It says essentially, "God would like to do something about the tragedies and evils that hurt us, but he just doesn't have the information." Both Rabbi Kushner's and Pastor Boyd's views try to make people feel better about their difficult life situations and about God himself. But sincere as they are, in the end, they hurt us a great deal more than they help.

Which divine attributes will we redefine next as a way of making us feel better about either our troubles or shortcomings? His omnipresence? His holiness? Whatever meager gains we suppose our revisions bring us, we end up with a god who has a lot more knowledge and power than us, but not enough to fully execute a loving plan for our lives.

God's promises are trustworthy.
I wince whenever a movie character leaves amid risky circumstances and promises a loved one "I'll be back" or "You'll be safe." The person means well but lacks the knowledge and power to keep that promise. God, however, in the biblical and orthodox understanding, does not have those limitations. Since nothing happens outside of God's sovereign control, Paul said with confidence, "I know whom I have believed, and *am convinced that he is able to guard what I have entrusted to him*" (2 Timothy 1:12). We can trust both God and his promises.

In *Trusting God,* Jerry Bridges wrote, "That which should distinguish the suffering of believers from unbelievers is the confidence that our suffering is under the control of an all-powerful and all-loving God. Our suffering has meaning and purpose in God's eternal plan, and He brings or allows to come into our lives only that which is for His glory and our good."[17]

Twenty-five years ago, on nine occasions I participated in peaceful, nonviolent civil disobedience, briefly going to jail in what was an extremely unpopular cause—speaking up for unborn children. Abortion clinics brought lawsuits against me and others. It seemed possible that if the lawsuits succeeded, we might lose our house and a good part of our monthly income.

During the three years we found ourselves in this stressful situation, Nanci and I would talk with our daughters—eight and ten when the legal problems began—assuring them that God remained in control, that he knew everything that would happen, and that we could trust him to use it for good.

Our daughters believed this and prayed with a kind of trust in God that still brings tears to my eyes. One night when an abortion clinic tried to drop us from a lawsuit (this required our permission, but our agreement might have helped their case), we asked our daughters, "What do you think God wants us to do?" Though they understood their answer might mean losing our house and leaving the private school they loved, my then twelve-year-old daughter said, as her sister and my wife nodded in agreement, "Daddy, if the abortion clinic doesn't want you there, I think God does."

We prayed together again; I called our attorney and spent the next month in court in one of the most difficult experiences of our lives. While our activities caused no actual damage to the clinics, except the money lost for abortions prevented, the jury found our group liable for $8.2 million in punitive damages.

My family faced this situation with the firm belief that God is all-knowing *and* all-powerful *and* all-loving, and that no matter what happened, he would work things out for our ultimate good.

And he did!

The fact that we lost the case was irrelevant. We've already seen how God has used this situation for good in countless ways, though no doubt we'll learn more when we're with him in eternity.

But suppose we had believed in open theism. Our conversations with our children would have been remarkably different: "Girls, we don't know how this lawsuit is going to turn out. We don't know if we'll lose our house. We don't know if you'll be able to continue in school. *And God doesn't know either.* God wishes the best for us, and he'll do what he can to help, but we can't know he has a definite purpose or plan in this, and there's no assurance that this will work out for our greatest good."

I cannot express how radically different our family's prayers and peace of mind would have been had we believed that. Instead, we believed what Scripture teaches about his omniscience and sovereign plan, and God helped us trust him and his purposes.

I take great comfort in the conviction that the Lord saw exactly what would happen in a world of human beings and fallen angels. He knew what the Fall would bring, and he saw from before the beginning how the ultimate good of manifesting his love and grace would bring an eternal richness to the universe.

If God had to do it all over again—knowing what he knows and has always known—he would create the same world, grant the same capacity to choose, and sovereignly permit the same evils while carrying out his plan of ultimate and eternal good for his children.

If the world's sufferings (and his own on the cross) are worth it to the all-knowing and sovereign God revealed to us in Scripture, then in the end without end, surely they will be worth it to us.

Notes

The second epigraph is from A. W. Tozer, *The Knowledge of the Holy* (San Francisco, CA: HarperOne, 1992), 87.

1. Clark Pinnock, "God Limits His Knowledge," in Feinberg et al., *Predestination and Free Will* (Downers Grove, IL: InterVarsity, 1986), 156.

2. Revelation 13:8 may be speaking instead about names written in the Book of Life before the world's foundation; if so, the notion of the absolute certainty of Christ's eventual redemptive work is still apparent in passages such as Acts 2:23; 4:27–28; 1 Peter 1:20.

3. Bruce A. Ware, *Their God Is Too Small: Open Theism and the Undermining of Confidence in God* (Wheaton, IL: Crossway Books, 2003), 32–34.

4. Wayne Grudem, *Systematic Theology: An Introduction to Biblical Doctrine* (Grand Rapids, MI: Zondervan, 1994), 164.

5. Gregory A. Boyd, *God of the Possible: A Biblical Introduction to the Open View of God* (Grand Rapids, MI: Baker, 2000), 102.

6. Boyd, *God of the Possible,* 98.

7. Pinnock, "God Limits His Knowledge," in Feinberg et al., *Predestination and Free Will,* 150.

8. Gregory A. Boyd, *Is God to Blame?* (Downers Grove, IL: InterVarsity, 2003), 110.

9. Boyd, *Is God to Blame?,* 13.

10. Boyd, *Is God to Blame?,* 16, 21.

11. Boyd, *God of the Possible,* 105–6.

12. A. H. Strong, *Outlines of Systematic Theology* (Philadelphia: Griffith and Roland, 1908), 77.

13. Ware, *Their God Is Too Small,* 16.

14. Gregory A. Boyd, "A Response to John Piper," May 4, 1998, www.bge .bethel.edu/4know/response.htm.

15. Paul Kjoss Helseth, "God Causes All Things," in Helseth et al., *Four Views on Divine Providence* (Grand Rapids, MI: Zondervan, 2011), 48.

16. Justin Taylor, introduction to *Beyond the Bounds: Open Theism and the Undermining of Biblical Christianity,* eds. John Piper, Justin Taylor, and Paul Kjoss Helseth (Wheaton, IL: Crossway Books, 2003), 13.

17. Jerry Bridges, *Trusting God: Even When Life Hurts* (Colorado Springs, CO: NavPress, 2008), 21.

The Fascinating Interplay of God's Sovereignty and Human Choice

Trust in the LORD with all your heart,
    and do not lean on your own understanding.
In all your ways acknowledge him,
    and he will make straight your paths.

Proverbs 3:5–6, ESV

In the Bible, divine sovereignty and human responsibility are not enemies. They are not uneasy neighbors; they are not in an endless state of cold war with each other. They are friends, and they work together.

J. I. Packer

God is free to exercise his sovereignty in ways of his choosing. Instead of imposing our preconceived notions or logical deductions on what sovereignty or free will should entail, we must let Scripture teach us what's true. That's why I devoted chapters to what God's Word says about both.

Christians who see human choice as holding more sway than God's choice need to reflect further on the Scripture in chapter 3. Those who see human choice as negated by God's sovereignty need to reflect further on the Scripture in chapter 4.

Hard determinism sees sovereignty not only as God's absolute power over evil and his ability to bring redemptive good out of it, but also as his detailed scripting and causation of every single thought and detail in all creation—including all evil, every lustful thought, each act of child abuse, and every holocaust. It may be a perfectly logical and self-consistent philosophy, but it omits or utterly reinterprets a significant part of the picture Scripture reveals: God-granted creature choices that fall completely under his sovereignty yet do not come out of his holy and loving heart.

It isn't accurate to say that anyone who believes in the significant power of human choice denies God's sovereignty. A king with full power over his armies may be called sovereign over his country. But when he grants his general the authority to make strategic battle choices, the king hasn't relinquished power; he has delegated it. Likewise, while God is sovereign over all things, he has granted meaningful and consequential choices to humans.

Nevertheless, it's easy to take too far this analogy with a human king. After all, God is not simply *called* sovereign in some figurative sense; he actually *is* Sovereign.

Paul calls God "he who is the blessed [Greek *makarios,* meaning "happy"] and only Sovereign, the King of kings and Lord of lords" (1 Timothy 6:15, ESV). Note that he's called the *only* Sovereign but not the only king; rather he is King of kings. The fact that human beings are called kings and lords, though only secondary ones, indicates his delegation of choice and power to humanity.

In this chapter, we'll further explore some points about God's sovereignty and human choice.

God sometimes overrules the most powerful human rulers.
On balance, Scripture indicates that people can and do make real, meaningful, and consequential choices, both bad and good. Yet it also makes clear that God sometimes chooses to overrule our choices.

His dealings with Pharaoh and Nebuchadnezzar are prime examples. In each case God chose arguably the most powerful human being on the planet as object lessons to show that no one has any power unless God chooses to grant it.

Isaiah's prophecy about Cyrus, the coming Persian ruler, is stunning in its scope. God calls him "my shepherd" and says that through him, he will "accomplish all that I please," including the rebuilding of Jerusalem and the temple (Isaiah 44:28; see 45:13).

> This is what the LORD says to his anointed,
>> to Cyrus, whose right hand I take hold of....
> For the sake of Jacob my servant,
>> of Israel my chosen,
> I summon you by name
>> and bestow on you a title of honor,
>> though you do not acknowledge me.
> I am the LORD, and there is no other;
>> apart from me there is no God. (Isaiah 45:1, 4–5)

Whether or not a human ruler acknowledges God, the Creator can use him however he wishes. The man may appear to make all his own choices, but the choices of God are, in this case, determining this ruler's choices. I find it difficult to reconcile this with the libertarian position.

Are Cyrus, Pharaoh, and the others exceptions? Apparently not: "The king's heart is a stream of water in the hand of the LORD; he turns it wherever he will" (Proverbs 21:1, ESV). Paul saw God working through Rome's ungodly government that would execute him: "He is God's servant for your good.... Who carries out God's wrath on the wrongdoer.... The authorities are ministers of God" (Romans 13:4, 6, ESV).

Scripture itself usually does not struggle with this paradox.
The biblical writers share some, but not all, of our theological dilemmas. Job, David, Habakkuk, and others raise the problem of evil and suffering. But they seem to struggle less with the notion that God's sovereign control would jeopardize human choice. To them, God has unlimited freedom.

It's biblically accurate to say that God's choices vastly outweigh human choices, since he is all-powerful and we are very limited in power. If this view represented only God's intrinsic power in contrast to that of his creatures (who have no intrinsic power, only what God has granted them), it would be perfect. But this view could also lead us logically to negate what the Bible says about meaningful human choice. It's absolutely true to say the Creator's choices are far weightier than his creatures' choices. But you cannot read the Bible without concluding that human choices really do matter.

> Satan doesn't care which side of the horse we fall off of, as long as we don't stay in the saddle.
>
> —Martin Luther

On the other hand, when our view of human choice leads us to believe that we or demons are in control, our weak and unbiblical view of God's sovereignty effectively shrinks God.

These two extreme views remind me of Martin Luther's statement that Satan doesn't care which side of the horse we fall off of, as long as we don't stay in the saddle. Hard determinism falls off one side; extreme libertarianism falls off the other.

The better we understand all the positions, the better able we are to establish our own.

My conversations with some Arminians suggest they believe that God's sovereignty, particularly in the area of our response to the gospel, must never encroach upon human will and actions. This is difficult to reconcile with Luke saying, "And as many as were ordained to eternal life believed" (Acts 13:48, KJV, RSV), and with Jesus saying, "All that the Father gives me will come to me" (John 6:37). Strict libertarianism at times seems to minimize God's sovereignty.

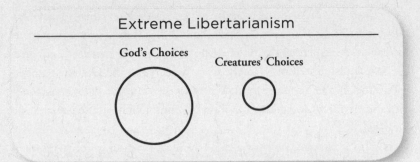

Extreme Libertarianism

God's Choices

Creatures' Choices

As a secular philosophy, libertarianism doesn't recognize God. But Christian libertarians, normally Arminians, acknowledge that God is greater than his creatures, and therefore his power, control, and choices are bigger and greater. Nonetheless, beyond the fact that he has granted them free choice, some Arminians see creature choices as existing outside of the circle of God's choices and, to a degree at least, outside his control (not his *theoretical* control, due to powerlessness, but his *actual* control, due to granting the power of contrary choice).

In the Christian libertarianism embraced by most Arminians, as portrayed in the next diagram, the portion of creatures' choices that overlaps God's choices is prevenient grace, the empowerment God gives humans to believe in him if they so choose. This is modified libertarianism.

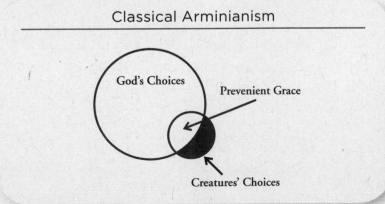

Classical Arminianism

God's Choices

Prevenient Grace

Creatures' Choices

Both Arminians and Calvinists recognize prevenient grace as a divine enabling of sinners to place their faith in God. When Augustine spoke of prevenient grace, or enabling grace, he considered it to be irresistible and granted only to the elect, which fits the Calvinist understanding. However, when John Wesley spoke of prevenient grace, he saw it as something God grants to all people, but which can be resisted and refused.

This is why I've portrayed the Arminian position in the diagram as having part of God's choice overlapping human choice. Prevenient grace, as understood by Wesley, belongs under God's choice since he chooses to extend it. Humans do not make the choice to receive prevenient grace; rather, God unilaterally gives it to all, allowing us to accept the gift of eternal life if we so choose. To those who respond to his grace-enabled invitation to believe, God unilaterally gives new birth.

The following diagrams illustrate compatibilism, the position that human free will is compatible with divine determinism. The circle of human choice, while real and meaningful and sometimes destructive, does not exist outside the purposeful governance of God. These are three different ways compatibilism could be depicted, depending on how they might be interpreted, as well as the varied perspectives of compatibilists. (As with the other positions, not all compatibilists are precisely alike in their thinking.)

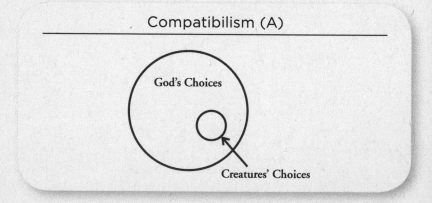

Compatibilism (A)

God's Choices

Creatures' Choices

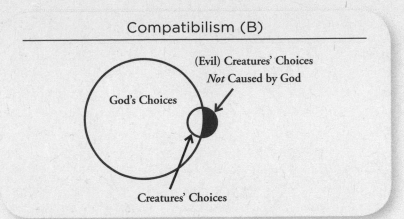

Compatibilism (B)

God's Choices

(Evil) Creatures' Choices
Not Caused by God

Creatures' Choices

Some compatibilists would be comfortable with the first diagram (A). Others would feel this better fits not their position but hard determinism, or hyper-Calvinism, since all creature choices appear subsumed by and indistinguishable from God's choices.

Those wishing to distinguish themselves from hyper-Calvinists might favor the second depiction (B), in which creature choices that are God honoring are empowered through God's choice to extend grace, while creature choices to commit evil lie outside of God's direct choice, falling instead under his choice to *allow* them. Hence, God permits evil but doesn't cause it.

I prefer the depiction on the following page, which comes closest to what I think Scripture as a whole reveals.

Note that God's choices and creature choices all exist within his sovereign rule. The evils done by God's creatures are their choices, not his. He chooses to permit evils—and could have prevented them—but he doesn't *cause* them; he's not the author of evil. Nonetheless, his creatures' wrong choices exist within his decree and the unlimited circle of his sovereignty, and they don't defeat his ultimate purpose and plan. He could have chosen to not permit them, and his permission reflects both purpose and plan. Indeed, he uses at least some of his creatures' disobedience, if not all of it, to accomplish that plan.

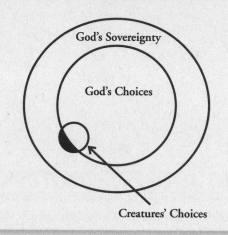

Compatibilism (C)

God's Sovereignty

God's Choices

Creatures' Choices

Some Arminians also believe that God remains 100 percent in control in his governance and that he will use all things, even evil, for the good of his people. In this respect they're similar to Calvinist compatibilists, who might feel that diagram C is close to what they believe. I would put A. W. Tozer in this category; he didn't want to call himself a Calvinist or an Arminian, but when you read him he sometimes sounds much like a compatibilist, though other times more like a libertarian tempered by a vast view of God and his sovereignty. He's emphatic that the reality and importance of human choice in no way inhibits God's sovereign control of all things.

The difference between the compatibilist view and the hyper-Calvinist view is seen in the next diagram.

Here, creatures' choices appear within the circle of God's choices, as they do in one of the compatibilist diagrams, but in this case it's illusory; it's the *appearance* of free choice but not the reality. For the hard determinist, the person makes choices only as dictated by God in every detail. The dummy on the lap of the ventriloquist appears to be thinking and choosing, but he isn't.

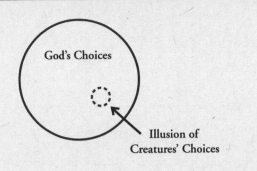

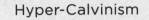

Which view on sovereignty and free will best explains the biblical paradox of God's decreed will differing from his moral will? It seems to me that violating the moral will of God requires meaningful human choice, while fulfilling the decreed will of God requires divine determinism. Since compatibilism entails both, I believe it has the greatest explanatory power. Hard determinism seems to deny meaningful choice, and libertarianism seems to so emphasize free choice that God's sovereign choices become secondary.

Hard determinism leaves no room for contrary choice, no matter how we define it. But by its affirmation of determinism's coexistence with meaningful choice, I believe compatibilism leaves room for limited or qualified contrary choice. Some compatibilists will take issue with this, but if contrary choice is understood as not involving autonomy or the ability to act contrary to one's nature, I believe it does not have to inhibit God's sovereignty or his ability to determine outcomes. "Choice" by definition involves selecting between alternatives. Compatibilists arguing against contrary choice sometimes appear to deny real choice, which compatibilism actually affirms. Compatibilists who minimize human choice sound like hyper-Calvinists. In any case, just as Arminianism is a big tent, so is Calvinism, one that agrees on some central issues while leaving room for disagreement on others.

Strengths and Weaknesses of Major Views

	Hyper-Calvinism (Hard Determinists)	Calvinism (Compatibilists)	Arminianism (Libertarians)	Molinism (Calvinists or Arminians)
Strengths	A clear position—no meaningful human choice. God's sovereignty is everything, free will nonexistent, so there's no problem or paradox to resolve.	Affirms man's choice and responsibility and God's control. No unnecessary suffering. God is actively orchestrating events to work for the good of his children, who make meaningful choices within creaturely limits.	Aligns with the human experience of free will, which seems obvious in daily life. Able to account for the extreme evil in the world. Suffering can't be blamed on God, though he allows it. God still seen as in control but not micro-managing evil.	Explains one way God could remain fully sovereign while allowing humans to exercise free will. Can be held by either Arminians (usually) or Calvinists.
Weaknesses	God is the author and source of all evil. He's behind each and every choice, and therefore	Believes in divine determinism and human free will. Since it can't reconcile them, at	Doesn't account for how God can control outcomes if he does not control creatures'	Can be believed by both libertarians and compatibilists, so its implications are

Weaknesses (cont.)	behind all evil choices. Does not adequately account for human choices opposed to God's will. If God's is the only will involved, choice is an illusion and human life a pretense. What's the point?	times it appears illogical or self-contradictory. Its emphasis on God's sovereignty makes it easy to pay only lip service to human choices, sometimes making it sound like Hyper-Calvinism.	choices. Affirms God's sovereignty but minimizes it, since human and demonic choices prevail. God is so distanced from human suffering that he appears to have empathy, but no purpose and plan.	unclear; doesn't fully qualify as a major alternative. Can't always affirm, "This is what a Molinist would say."
Biblical Support	Deuteronomy 32:39; Proverbs 16:33; Isaiah 45:5–7; Lamentations 3:37–38; Romans 9:19–22	Genesis 50:20; Proverbs 21:1; Isaiah 44:28; John 6:44; Acts 2:23	Deuteronomy 30:19; Joshua 24:14–15; Isaiah 1:19–20; Matthew 23:37; John 12:32; James 1:13	1 Samuel 23:10–12; Matthew 11:21–24; 1 Corinthians 2:7–8

God's sovereignty requires absolute governance, but believers debate whether it requires absolute control.

Just because someone doesn't believe God actively intervenes to cause every thought and action, including evil ones, doesn't mean he doesn't believe in God's sovereignty. Arminian theologian Jack Cottrell wrote, "A sovereign God is a God who is free to limit himself with regard to his works, a God who is free to decide not to determine if he so chooses, a God who is free to bestow the gift of relative independence upon his creatures. Such freedom does not diminish God's sovereignty; it magnifies it."[1]

When I was an Arminian, I believed God *could* overrule human will, and I believed he sometimes *did*. That God is all-powerful and absolutely just doesn't mean he must in all moments fully exercise all his power to bring about justice. In his patience he delays the unleashing of judgment (see 2 Peter 3:9). All orthodox believers, Calvinists and Arminians alike, believe that Christ in some sense temporarily restricted the exercise of some of his divine attributes in the incarnation. That truth is attested to both by Philippians 2:7—which tells us that Jesus "emptied himself, by taking the form of a servant, being born in the likeness of men" (ESV)—and by Christ's statement in Matthew 24:36 that he didn't know the day or hour of his return.

A father who allows his children to play alone in the yard, where they'll potentially fall from a swing or fight with each other, doesn't lack power to control his children. He simply chooses not to, believing he's acting in his children's best interests. Obviously the human father doesn't know exactly what will happen as a result of giving his children limited freedom—while God does. Yet an all-powerful being is perfectly capable of permitting choices contrary to what pleases him. You cannot view the Bible or even the nightly news without seeing that God does act this way.

Some passages seem to indicate God's broad allowance of human choice, including human sin that he does not cause, prevent, or stop. (As a compatibilist, I believe he does this with purpose and plan in mind.) Some passages show that God directly and actively intervenes to control the details of life, even those that involve suffering. Some Calvinists may struggle with the predominance of human choices seen in Scripture and in life, some Arminians with the biblical statements that God controls life details that include even suffering. I believe God calls upon us to believe both.

The world is full of things that displease God.

When Scripture says our all-powerful God does whatever he pleases (see Psalm 115:3), it's easy to draw the wrong conclusion. After all, if *we* were all-powerful and did whatever we pleased (perish the thought), wouldn't we make a universe in which everything pleases us all the time? However, God was grieved by the world's great sins in the days of Noah (see Genesis 6:6). He was angered by Moses's reluctance to obey him (see Exodus 4:13–14). When David committed adultery and arranged the murder of Uriah, "the thing that David had done displeased the LORD" (2 Samuel 11:27).

> Since God does whatever he pleases, it must please him to permit people, for the present, to displease him!

God is displeased when his people choose sin: "Cast away from you all the transgressions that you have committed, and make yourselves a new heart and a new spirit! Why will you die, O house of Israel? For I have no pleasure in the death of anyone, declares the Lord GOD; so turn, and live" (Ezekiel 18:31–32, ESV). Notice that God does not negate or override his people's wills. Rather, he calls upon them to *choose* to repent of their sinful *choices*.

Jesus said God is displeased by our refusal to forgive (see Matthew 18:34–35). After their objections to him healing a man's shriveled hand in the synagogue on the Sabbath, Jesus was angry with the Pharisees and "grieved at their hardness of heart" (Mark 3:5, ESV).

Since God does whatever he pleases, it must please him to permit people, for the present, to displease him! The fact that God does whatever he pleases doesn't prove that it pleases him to determine every thought and action. It may please him more to determine that his image-bearers can make real choices compatible with his sovereignty.

Why does the all-powerful God tolerate wrong choices? Partly because he knows it will lead to a redemptive end that will please him more.[2]

A world of freedom requires cause and effect.
Many of us like the idea of the freedom to choose. We like its role in the development of human culture's best accomplishments. But we don't like the part it has played in humanity's worst moments.

For choice to be real, it must be effectual. Would you like to live in a world where every possibility of evil and pain was eliminated? Are you *sure*? C. S. Lewis invited us to imagine a world so structured that wooden beams would become "soft as grass" when used as weapons and that sound waves would not "carry lies or insults":

> But such a world would be one in which wrong actions were
> impossible, and in which, therefore, freedom of the will would
> be void;...evil thoughts would be impossible, for the cerebral
> matter which we use in thinking would refuse its task when we
> attempted to frame them.... Try to exclude the possibility of
> suffering which the order of nature and the existence of free
> wills involve, and you find that you have excluded life itself.[3]

In fact, the evil and suffering of this world are compatible with a God who despises evil but values freedom. If God did not permit the consequences of human choices, including the bad ones, this world would be one where people were content to do evil and tolerate it, feeling no need to turn to God. In such a world, people would die without a sense of need, only to find themselves in Hell.

Peter van Inwagen wrote, "If God simply 'canceled' all the horrors of this world by an endless series of miracles, he would thereby frustrate his own plan of reconciliation. If he did that, we should be content with our lot and should see no reason to cooperate with him."[4]

In this fallen world we can't influence each other for good unless we can also influence each other for evil. If I could not hurt you, I could not help you. If you could not kill me, you could not die for me.

If we say we wish God had made humans without the freedom to do evil, we're saying we don't think humans should have freedom, which is to say that humans shouldn't be human.

God is the potter and we are the clay, yet the clay makes choices. Some Scripture could lead us to believe—and has certainly led hard determinists (and some compatibilists, judging by their language) to believe—that we're only raw materials in God's hands. For instance, God says, "Behold, like the clay in the potter's hand, so are you in my hand, O house of Israel" (Jeremiah 18:6, ESV). This isn't a favorite memory verse of libertarians, any more than "Choose for yourselves this day whom you will serve" (Joshua 24:15) is a favorite of determinists.

> The evil and suffering of this world fit a
> God who despises evil but values freedom.

However, Jeremiah 18:11 continues, "Thus says the LORD, Behold, I am shaping disaster against you and devising a plan against you. Return, every one from his evil way, and amend your ways and your deeds" (ESV).

God sees their choice to sin, promises judgment, but calls upon them to abandon their old ways and choose new ones. He laments in verse 12, "But they say, 'That is in vain! We will follow our own plans, and will every one act according to the stubbornness of his evil heart'" (ESV).

At that point, God doesn't argue, "You can't follow your plans; you can only follow what I've planned for you."

Potters don't talk to their clay, at least not seriously. They don't call upon their clay to repent. God made Adam from the ground, and perhaps that's part of being clay. Whatever he means beyond that—and surely it includes his right to make of us whatever he wishes—it does *not* mean that we're inanimate clumps devoid of intelligence, will, or the ability to choose. (No more than calling us sheep means we're woolly and have four legs.)

God beseeches his people to repent. He's not telling us we can't choose or that our choices are meaningless, but that if we keep choosing evil and fail to turn from it, he'll judge us severely. This potter-and-clay passage totally affirms God's sovereignty, but it does not teach that God fulfills his plan by making us choose evil. (We do that effectively on our own, without his help.) He calls upon us to repent and choose him. When we sin, it's because we act in accordance with our sin natures.

> Does life have a meaningful purpose if it's nothing more than a scripted screenplay acted out on the stage of the universe?

Don't get me wrong. If God wanted to do so, he is fully capable of being a puppet master, sovereignly pulling every string of every creature in his universe to do exactly what he wants, all the time. That view of reality appears to be supported by some Scripture passages taken in isolation. But such a view is not taught by the larger context of the whole of Scripture—nor by our human experience.

Does life have a meaningful purpose if it's nothing more than a scripted screenplay acted out on the stage of the universe? (And one in which the actors don't even know they're acting?) It's always good to balance our talk of human choices with a reminder of God's sovereignty. Paul anticipates our natural response to his argument for God's sovereignty and election: "One of you will say to me: 'Then why does God still blame us? For who resists his will?' But who are you, O man, to talk back to God? 'Shall what is formed say to him who formed it, "Why did you make me like this?"' Does not the potter have the right to make out of the same lump of clay some pottery for noble purposes and some for common use?" (Romans 9:19–21). Scripture appeals here to *God's* free will, not man's; to the *Creator's* rights, not the creatures'.

And lest we think that calling himself the potter and us the clay is merely playing God, we should remember that God doesn't *play* God. He *is* God.

Every page of Scripture assumes our choices are both real and significant—they matter to God and should matter to us.

Our judicial system holds people accountable for their choices. A lawyer knows it's futile to argue, "He couldn't help killing that woman." Arguing determinism is morally abhorrent *and* logically absurd.

If we're at our child's sports-awards banquet, what would we think if someone announced, "There will be no awards this year for most improved, MVP, or sportsmanship, since those who worked harder than others had no choice but to do so; it was all predetermined"?

The implications of this issue are far reaching. If we have no ability to make one choice rather than another, why bother with life? Why seek to repent of sin if repenting (or not repenting) is entirely outside our control? In what way could I grow in conformity to Christ if my choices to read his Word, pray, seek fellowship, and resist temptation are not mine to make in the first place?

Arminians who agree with me on these points should remember there's another side to this. Scripture does use the term "predestined" (Acts 4:28, ESV; Romans 8:29–30; Ephesians 1:5, 11). Those who argue against God determining events should ask, "Am I arguing against the biblical doctrine of predestination?" Arminians do have a doctrine of predestination, which I referenced earlier, but should ask themselves whether it stands up fully to the biblical evidence.

The human will could fall only because it was free.

The story of the Fall is presented straightforwardly in Genesis 3:1–7 and taken at face value in the New Testament (see Romans 5:12–21). There was the initial choice of disobedience, which could only be made because God granted humanity free will.

In Christian theology, what God has ordained is called his *decree*. There are direct decrees and permissive decrees. The incarnation of

Christ is a direct decree, while the fall of Adam and Eve is an indirect or permissive decree. God didn't make sin happen, in the sense that he made the incarnation happen. He didn't merely permit the incarnation; he caused it. Permission and causation are not the same. Yet, God decreed both the sin he permitted and the incarnation he caused.

When some say God "determines" all things, they mean he intervenes directly, making sin happen just as he did the incarnation or as he makes the sun rise. Others use the same terminology but see God as never being the author of sin, never causing sin. Knowing the inclinations of human hearts, he governs their circumstances so that their own choices, freely made, fulfill his predetermined plan. This is one distinction between hyper-Calvinists and mainstream Calvinists, or compatibilists.

Adam and Eve possessed wills by which they could have chosen either to obey or disobey God. Until they disobeyed, they chose, for no matter how short or long a time, to obey. No understanding of what happened in Eden is possible without believing they were endowed by God with true and meaningful choice.

Meaningful choice is essential for genuine love.

There are many ways to define *love*. Suppose we define it as "an ongoing and ever-growing sense of deep personal affection and loyalty toward another." Even if you define it differently, can real love—in the sense of a meaningful, mutual relationship—exist without freedom?

Suppose that through threats, drugs, or hypnotism, I could coerce my wife to love me. (For the record, I haven't used any of these.) First, it would be a contradiction in terms. Her "loving" words and actions would be an illusion. I don't want to force her to love me, and if I somehow did, her "love" would not be love at all. I want her to love me simply because she wants to. Love requires the freedom not to love.

This is a fatal flaw in hyper-Calvinism. If God "makes" people love him by coercive determination, then of what value to God is their so-called love?

Even voluntary love needs to come out of more than a sense of duty. Here's an illustration adapted from John Piper.[5] Suppose that, on his wedding anniversary, a husband comes home from work with a stunning bouquet of flowers for his wife. As soon as he enters the front door, his wife exclaims, "Oh, honey, those are *gorgeous*! Thank you *so* much!" Immediately the husband replies, "No big deal. It's my duty."

How do you suppose the wife will receive this kind of "love"? Not with warmth, I guarantee you. (Don't try this at home!) People want to be loved out of true appreciation for who they are.

Isn't that also the sort of love God values? True, he doesn't *need* our love; but I'm talking about the kind of love he values.

In the movie *The Stepford Wives*, husbands program "perfect" wives, in the sense that they'll do whatever their husbands want. But what men really desire, despite the difficulties it brings, is a relationship with a real person who responds as she chooses. When she says "Thanks" or "I love you" or laughs at his jokes or kisses him, she really *means* it. Robotic or programmed love is cheap and empty, and indeed it's no love at all. If we can see the difference, surely God can see it far better.

This is one of my concerns when I read the arguments of those who profess to believe in human choice but affirm God's complete control of all human thoughts and actions, down to the smallest elements. I agree with much, even most of what they say about God's sovereignty, but taken to its logical conclusions, they come up with a picture I simply don't see in Scripture. What I see is a God who wants us to love him genuinely through his empowerment. But this isn't the same as him comprehensively programming or dictating our loving response to him. Can programmed or dictated love be love in any meaningful sense?

If poor choices weren't possible, there would be no "us."

When I think about the reality of choice, my mind goes to the movie *Indiana Jones and the Last Crusade*. After one of the bad guys chooses to drink out of the cup that will supposedly make him live forever, his skin melts, he becomes a skeleton, and he turns to dust. The guardian of the Holy Grail calmly observes, "He chose poorly." While the stakes of most of our choices are not so high, the stakes of our choices about the true source of eternal life are high indeed.

In a question-and-answer session with teenagers at my church, one student asked me, "Why doesn't God just overrule our choices whenever we're about to hurt ourselves or someone else?"

My eyes fell on two students I'd coached that week at the district tennis tournament. "Suppose," I said, "I had the power to keep Ryan and Stefan from making any choices that would hurt them. And suppose I had the power to keep anyone else from making choices that would hurt Ryan and Stefan. Should I do it?"

Many heads nodded. The obvious answer seemed to be yes.

"But it's not so simple," I continued. "I value Stefan and Ryan because they're individuals with their own personalities, qualities, and abilities. A fundamental part of their identity is their ability to make choices that have consequences. If I intervened to stop Stefan and Ryan from making hurtful decisions, in the end I wouldn't be protecting Stefan and Ryan. I would save them from evil and suffering, but they would lose their freedom and become incapable of maturing. They would no longer *be* the people I value."

In fact, if God protected us from all poor choices, he wouldn't be protecting us, because there would be no "us."

Isn't that too high a price to pay?

In Heaven and in the resurrection, we'll have free will but without the possibility of sin.

Some people argue that if true human freedom in Eden required the ability to choose evil, then either we won't be free in Heaven or we'll be able to sin again.

A sinless environment doesn't rule out the possibility of sin; Adam and Eve proved that. Before Satan sinned, he too was originally a good being living in a perfect environment. Hence, Heaven's perfection, it seems, doesn't in itself guarantee the absence of future sin.

Yet the Bible is clear: though we'll have freedom to choose in Heaven, we'll have no ability to sin. Christ promises that on the New Earth "there will be no more death or mourning or crying or pain" (Revelation 21:4).

Since "the wages of sin is death" (Romans 6:23), the promise of no more death requires that there be no more sin.

Consider the last part of Revelation 21:4, which is a future statement of Christ at the dawn of the New Earth: "For the old order of things has passed away." When the old order has passed away, we need not fear another Fall.

Scripture emphasizes that Christ died *once* to deal with sin and will never again need to die (see Hebrews 9:26–28; 10:10; 1 Peter 3:18). We'll have the full experience of our new nature, so that in Christ we will "become the righteousness of God" (2 Corinthians 5:21). Possessing God's own righteousness, we won't sin in Heaven for the same reason God doesn't: he *cannot*.

> Free will in Heaven will not require that we be capable of sinning or that humanity may fall again.

Christ purchased with his blood our eternal inability to sin: "For by a single offering [himself] he has perfected *for all time* those who are being sanctified" (Hebrews 10:14, ESV). To be perfected for all time demands that we never sin again.

Even in the present Heaven, prior to the resurrection, people cannot sin, for they are "the spirits of the righteous made perfect" (Hebrews 12:23, ESV). Ultimately, we'll be raised "incorruptible" (1 Corinthians 15:52, NKJV). *Incorruptible* is a stronger word than *uncorrupted*. While we'll have true freedom in Heaven, it will be a righteous freedom that never sins. Christ will not allow us to become vulnerable to the very thing he died to deliver us from (see Romans 4:25). Since our righteousness comes from Christ, who is eternally righteous, we'll never lose it (see Romans 5:19).

What does this mean in terms of human freedom? Once we become what the sovereign God has made us to be in Christ, and once we see him as he is, then we'll see all things—including sin—for what they are. *God won't need to restrain us from evil.* It will have absolutely no appeal. It will be, literally, unthinkable. The memory of evil and suffering in this life will serve as an eternal reminder of sin's horrors and emptiness.

Paul Helm said, "The freedom of heaven, then, is the freedom from sin; not that the believer just happens to be free from sin, but that he is so constituted or reconstituted that he cannot sin. He doesn't want to sin, and he does not want to want to sin."[6]

Meanwhile, as we look forward to the day when every choice will be righteous, God is not only preparing a place for us; he is, through our trust and suffering and character growth, preparing us for that place (see 2 Peter 3:11–14).

The God of the Bible is big enough to still be sovereign while granting real choice to his creatures.

Alvin Plantinga's influential free-will defense[7] is a proposed solution to help us understand the nature of our choices in a fallen world. Plantinga said,

> A world containing creatures who are significantly free (and freely perform more good than evil actions) is more valuable, all else being equal, than a world containing no free creatures at all. Now God can create free creatures, but He can't cause or determine them to do only what is right. For if He does so, then they aren't significantly free after all; they do not do what is right freely. To create creatures capable of moral good, therefore, He must create creatures capable of moral evil; and He can't give these creatures the freedom to perform evil and at the same time prevent them from doing so. As it turned out, sadly enough, some of the free creatures God created went wrong in the exercise of their freedom; this is the source of moral evil.[8]

Though many people think the free-will argument gives the best response to the problem of evil, it doesn't seem to me that the value of human freedom of choice could alone outweigh all the world's suffering and evil.

Another approach, the greater-good argument, seems more compelling and springs directly from the Bible (see, for example, Romans 8:18; 2 Corinthians 4:17). In fact, the building of Christlike character alone might be enough to outweigh evil and suffering, as might be the eternally celebrated unveiling of God's grace in redemption.

But could the greater-good argument itself work without meaningful choice? Without it, could we have a significant relationship with God? The greatest commandment is that we love God with our whole beings (see Matthew 22:37). Could we do that without being capable of meaningful choice?

I would put it this way: The God of the Scriptures is so big, wise, and powerful that he can grant truly meaningful and real choices to angels and humans alike, in a way that allows them to act freely, within their finite limits, without inhibiting his sovereign plan in any way—and indeed using their meaningful choices, even their disobedience, in a significant way to *fulfill* his sovereign plan.

Had God wished to, he could easily have constructed a world where Adam and Eve had true choice yet never succumbed to sin. Of course, there would have been no Fall, but there would also have been no redemption, no manifestation of the saving grace of God. So God instead put them in circumstances where the exercise of their free choice would result in sin. Yet it also resulted in the redemptive work of Christ, including his incarnation and resurrection, and his eventual return to resurrect his children and re-create the universe itself.

Choice is a bittersweet gift. Those in Heaven will always be grateful they had it and will have it always, with no fear of sin or condemnation; those in Hell will always regret that they didn't exercise it differently.

Notes

The second epigraph is from J. I. Packer, *Evangelism and the Sovereignty of God* (Downers Grove, IL: InterVarsity, 1961), 40.

1. Jack Cottrell, *What the Bible Says About God the Ruler* (Eugene, OR: Wipf and Stock, 2000), 217.

2. For a detailed treatment of the problem of evil and suffering, see my book *If God Is Good* (Colorado Springs, CO: Multnomah, 2009) or the smaller volume *The Goodness of God* (Colorado Springs, CO: Multnomah, 2010).

3. C. S. Lewis, *The Problem of Pain,* in *The Complete C. S. Lewis Signature Classics* (New York: HarperCollins, 2002), 565.

4. Peter van Inwagen, *Christian Faith and the Problem of Evil* (Grand Rapids, MI: Eerdmans, 2004), 71.

5. John Piper, "Worship: The Feast of Christian Hedonism," Desiring God, September 25, 1983, www.desiringgod.org/sermons/worship-the-feast -of-christian-hedonism.

6. Paul Helm, *The Last Things* (Carlisle, PA: Banner of Truth, 1989), 92.

7. See Alvin Plantinga, *God, Freedom, and Evil* (Grand Rapids, MI: Eerdmans, 1974).

8. Plantinga, *God, Freedom, and Evil,* 30.

Meaningful Human Choice and Divine Sovereignty Working hand in Hand

Look now; I myself am he!
>   There is no other god but me!
I am the one who kills and gives life;
>   I am the one who wounds and heals;
>   no one can be rescued from my powerful hand!

Deuteronomy 32:39, NLT

I know why I am here and my only real focused goal is to live each day to the fullest and to try and honor God and be an encouragement to others. What the future holds is firmly in God's hands, and I am very happy about that!

Ken Hensley

I love underwater photography and have spent hundreds of hours enjoying God's undersea world. I've watched, fascinated, as giant sea turtles wait at their "cleaning stations," while various colorful fish, with surgical precision, remove edible parasites and algae from creatures fifty to a hundred times their size. The turtles could easily snap the little fish in two. But they don't. They know the fish help them, just as they help the fish. Similarly, cleaner shrimp enter the jaws of ferocious eels who could swallow them whole. But again, they don't. God created these unlikely symbiotic relationships.

Divine sovereignty and human choice are another unlikely duo. You would think that God's sovereignty would swallow human choice whole. (In some worldviews, it does.) Yet somehow, in Scripture, we see that despite the fact that God doesn't need us, he allows his infinitely greater will to interact cooperatively with our tiny lesser wills in a sort of symbiotic union—one in which we, it would seem, are the only true beneficiaries. Yet, incredibly, God himself, not needing us but loving us, takes pleasure in the relationship too:

> The LORD will again rejoice over you for good, just as He rejoiced over your fathers. (Deuteronomy 30:9, NASB)

> I will rejoice in doing them good. (Jeremiah 32:41)

> The LORD your God is in your midst,
>   a mighty one who will save;
> he will rejoice over you with gladness;
>   he will quiet you by his love;
> he will exult over you with loud singing.
>   (Zephaniah 3:17, ESV)

God's freedom and ours can be compared to a ship crossing the ocean.

Every analogy falls short, but this one can be adapted to reflect a variety of views.

A hard determinist sees humans walking about the ship appearing to freely choose, yet they're really preprogrammed automatons with no true freedom. Some are destined to clean the decks; some are stuck in the engine rooms. Some will enjoy the luxury rooms, while others will steal purses. There's no permission; everything's mandated. Meaningful human choice is illusory.

The extreme libertarian envisions herself as fully free not only to roam the ship and do whatever she wishes, but to get off this ship and captain her own, sailing to any harbor she chooses.

Compatibilists and moderate libertarians would both say the passengers have freedom to walk the ship, to choose when and where and what to eat, whether or not to befriend others, and whether to act kindly or with malice. Compatibilists would say there are more limits on passenger freedom than libertarians imagine. Perhaps the captain enforces certain restrictions. Being in bondage to sin might be analogous to having disabilities that would prevent passengers from accessing certain parts of the ship.

What no passenger can do is change the course of the ship; the owner, who's also the captain, makes that decision. Furthermore, unlike any human being, God controls the weather and knows where the icebergs are. He'll bring his ship into harbor where and when he wants.

Meanwhile unbelievers and believers alike are passengers able to make real choices, living under God's rules. We can have dinner with the captain or volunteer to work. We may also attempt mutiny—and may appear momentarily to have our way. But we won't succeed. The ship owner and captain is, in anything analogous to the Bible, omnipotent. When the ship reaches its predetermined destination, we'll be held accountable for our actions.

Using his own ship illustration, A. W. Tozer said, "Both freedom and sovereignty are present here and they do not contradict each other. So it is, I believe, with man's freedom and the sovereignty of God. The mighty liner of God's sovereign design keeps its steady course over the sea of history. God moves undisturbed and unhindered toward the fulfillment of those eternal purposes which He purposed in Christ Jesus before the world began."[1]

God's choices are at work, intermingling with ours in our daily lives.

The Westminster Confession of 1646 carefully affirms both God's will and the human will:

> God from all eternity did by the most wise and holy counsel of his own will, freely and unchangeably ordain whatsoever comes to pass; yet so as thereby neither is God the author of sin; nor is violence offered to the will of creatures; nor is the liberty or contingency of second causes taken away, but rather established.[2]

God's will is primary, ours is secondary; but both are real, and both have consequences. Deny the primacy of God's choices or the value of our choices, and you deny the Christian faith.

Deism isn't a worldview option for Christians, but has relevance to the sovereignty and choice discussion. I want to use deism to clarify by contrast what a biblical worldview looks like, in terms of a God who chooses and acts, while interrelating with human image-bearers who choose and act.

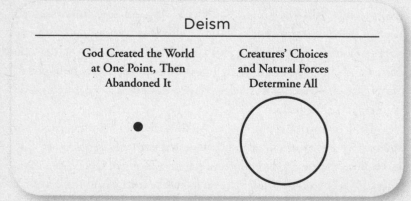

Far more people than are familiar with the term *deist* are, in fact, deists. They credit God with creating the universe, but have no concept of God exercising influence, much less sovereignty, in this world. Most deists don't think about angelic beings either. They suppose the only significant choices in this world are made by humans.

To them, God made the world, wound it up like a clock, and left this universe to run itself because he had better things to do. We're left to fend for ourselves—the power of our choices is what we have working for us. There's no walking hand in Hand with the God of deism, whose philosophy is "hands off." (Remember, the God of deism doesn't actually exist any more than Zeus does—he's a human construct very different than the true God of the Bible.)

There are polytheists, pantheists, and other kinds of theists, but most monotheists believe in a God who, at least theoretically, is an active participant in the world. The God of the Bible, in stark contrast to the God of deism, is dynamically engaged with this world, not only sustaining it, but governing in providence, intervening with miracles, taking deliberate actions, and accomplishing his plan.

What could be called hyper-libertarianism is the opposite danger of hyper-determinism (hyper-Calvinism). Not only does it make us see God as less of a difference maker; it easily drifts into a deistic way of looking at life. God, while present in the hearts of his people, is seen as not actively engaged in influencing the course of world events or purposefully directing the choices of his creatures. If demons and humans control the course of my life through their choices, God is effectively absent. It's as if things have spun so out of control that until Christ returns, he's given up. I can ask him to intervene, but if he regards human freedom of choice and the natural order as sacred, would he willingly interfere with either to answer my prayers?

From the beginning, Scripture lays out the story of human choices.

Scripture uses forms of the word *choose* hundreds of times, referring both to humans and God. To deny the reality of human choice is to deny our nature as God's image bearers.

God is an intelligent being who makes meaningful choices, all of them right. We are intelligent beings who make meaningful choices, both right and wrong. Our choices have far less impact than God's, since we're so much less consequential than God. Still, our choices are important.

Our inclination to choose righteously was marred in the Fall, after which there was a downward moral spiral: "The LORD saw that the wickedness of man was great in the earth, and that every intention of the thoughts of his heart was only evil continually" (Genesis 6:5, ESV).

Nevertheless, under the Old Covenant, God regularly calls upon his people to make good choices. Most of these passages seem to assume that his people are capable, *with his help,* of doing so. He said to Israel, "I have set before you life and death, blessing and curse. Therefore choose life, that you and your offspring may live" (Deuteronomy 30:19, ESV). Later, his spokesman Joshua told them, "Choose this day whom you will serve.... But as for me and my house, we will serve the LORD" (Joshua 24:15, ESV). Had the Israelites protested, "We don't have the strength to choose to serve God," Joshua would likely have responded, "No, by yourself you don't. But when God commands us to serve him, he can grant us the power to do so. Turn to him for help!"

> God is an intelligent being who makes meaningful choices, all of them right.

When God's people chose false gods, they were told they'd have to live with the inabilities of those gods: "Go and cry out to the gods whom you have chosen; let them save you in the time of your distress" (Judges 10:14, ESV).

Jesus said to Martha, "Mary has chosen the good portion, which will not be taken away from her" (Luke 10:42, ESV). Mary, in choosing to sit at Jesus' feet, had chosen wisely. Jesus encouraged Martha to do the same.

Biblical characters are often said to have made choices. Even where the words *choose* or *choice* aren't used, choices are everywhere in Scripture's storyline. Randomly flip through the Bible, stop at a page, and read, and you'll find someone making choices, even if it's the inspired author choosing to speak about God and his ways.

We're to choose to fear God (see Proverbs 1:29). Solomon encouraged his son, "Do not envy a man of violence and do not choose any of his ways" (Proverbs 3:31, ESV). Moses is commended for "choosing rather to be mistreated with the people of God than to enjoy the fleeting pleasures of sin" (Hebrews 11:25, ESV).

God determines the outworking of his plans, while granting us small-scale choices. What is choice but the ability to determine? If we lack that ability, then "compatibilism" is a nonsensical term—there's nothing for divine determinism to be compatible *with* if not effectual creature choices. God delegated to Adam and Eve responsibilities, for example, to determine animals' names. God sovereignly determines (chooses) to give us limited determination (choice).

Many biblical references emphasize God's freedom of choice.

Often we don't think about God as a choice-maker, but that's who he is and what he does, and why those made in his image are choice-makers.

The phrase "the LORD will choose" appears seven times in Deuteronomy. God said to Israel, "The LORD your God has chosen you to be a people for his treasured possession." He explained: "It was not because you were more in number than any other people that the LORD set his love on you and chose you, for you were the fewest of all peoples" (Deuteronomy 7:6–7, ESV).

God said, "I have chosen Jerusalem that my name may be there, and I have chosen David to be over my people Israel" (2 Chronicles 6:6, ESV).

David said, "Blessed is the one you choose and bring near, to dwell in your courts!" (Psalm 65:4, ESV). Jesus chose the twelve apostles (see Luke 6:13). Judas was chosen as an apostle yet not among God's chosen (see John 13:18).

The apostles might have felt they chose Jesus. Yet he said, "*You did not choose me, but I chose you* and appointed you" (John 15:16).

Jesus said to his followers, "I have chosen you out of the world" (verse 19). God's people are "the elect, whom he has chosen" (Mark 13:20). Jesus said, "For many are called, but few are chosen" (Matthew 22:14, ESV).

James 2:5 says, "Listen, my beloved brothers, has not God chosen those who are poor in the world to be rich in faith and heirs of the kingdom, which he has promised to those who love him?" (ESV). Paul wrote, "Put on then, *as God's chosen ones,* holy and beloved, compassionate hearts, kindness, humility, meekness, and patience" (Colossians 3:12, ESV). He and Peter saw God as choosing the believer:

> For we know, brothers loved by God, that he has chosen you.
> (1 Thessalonians 1:4)
>
> You are a chosen race. (1 Peter 2:9, ESV)
>
> God chose you as the firstfruits to be saved, through sanctification by the Spirit and belief in the truth. (2 Thessalonians 2:13, ESV)
>
> [God] chose us in him before the foundation of the world.
> (Ephesians 1:4, ESV)

We're accustomed to thinking highly of our God-given choices. We would do well to contemplate God's remarkable choices to select us before the world began, to deliver us from sin and death, and to allow us to live with him in everlasting happiness.

Jesus told his disciples, who were thrilled to cast out demons, "Do not rejoice that the spirits submit to you, but rejoice that your names are written in heaven" (Luke 10:20). *We* have not written our names in Heaven—*God* has. That God chose me to be his child, despite my unworthiness, is the greatest of all causes of celebration.

God's sovereignty and meaningful choice are both woven into Scripture.

D. A. Carson groups Scripture passages affirming God's sovereignty under four headings:

1. God is the creator, ruler, and possessor of all things.
2. God is the ultimate personal cause of all that happens.

3. God elects his people.
4. God is the unacknowledged source of good fortune or success.[3]

Then, under the following nine headings, Carson groups passages demonstrating that people are free and responsible moral agents:

1. People face a multitude of divine exhortations and commands.
2. People obey, believe, and choose God.
3. People sin and rebel against God.
4. People's sins are judged by God.
5. People are tested by God.
6. People receive divine rewards.
7. The elect are responsible to respond to God's initiative.
8. Prayers are not mere showpieces scripted by God.
9. God literally pleads with sinners to repent and be saved.[4]

Taken by themselves, the first group of four statements, particularly "God is the ultimate personal cause of all that happens," seems to preclude most of the second group's nine. But Carson isn't stating these points based on taking any one of them to its logical conclusions, but strictly on what Scripture actually reveals.

Part of the value of this list is its demonstration of what it looks like when we let Scripture speak for itself. I believe Carson's summary is accurate and serves as a biblical checklist any worldview needs to pass. Any position that does justice to the first four components and not the last nine is misguided. Any that addresses the last nine but doesn't embrace the first four also fails as a biblical worldview. It's easy to see (for everyone but its proponents, perhaps) that hyper-Calvinism doesn't do justice to the second nine. Libertarians, whether classical Arminians or open theists, need to evaluate whether their worldview stands up to the first four. Compatibilists should examine whether their worldview truly embraces and accounts for all the points in both lists.

God's sovereignty is consistent with human responsibility.

"If a man is lazy," says Ecclesiastes, "the rafters sag; if his hands are idle, the house leaks" (10:18). Proverbs 20:4 says, "A sluggard does not plow in season; so at harvest time he looks but finds nothing." These verses don't attribute sagging rafters and leaking houses to God's sovereignty. They lay responsibility for action on us. Though the sovereign God easily could, he refuses to do for us what he wants us to do.

Students who don't study and refuse to set an alarm to get up for class aren't trusting God; they're being irresponsible. It's consistent to believe in God's sovereignty and yet lock the door at night.

The book of Nehemiah records God's sovereign plan to rebuild Jerusalem. Yet it repeatedly shows Nehemiah preparing and strategically positioning the people to counter the many enemies opposed to the rebuilding of the city walls: "We prayed to our God and posted a guard day and night to meet this threat" (4:9). They prayed, recognizing God's sovereignty, and also posted a guard, recognizing their responsibility to choose wisely.

No contradiction exists between praying, "Lord, please protect us," and then fastening our seat belts. Prayers for healing don't conflict with medical treatment. Carl Sagan wrote, "We can pray over the cholera victim, or we can give her 500 milligrams of tetracycline every 12 hours."[5] But why should we choose between the two? Believers understand that praying for the sick before, after, and while giving medicine helps them in vital ways.

The apostle Paul labored to spread Christ's gospel. At one point he nodded toward the other apostles and wrote, "I worked harder than all of them." But he quickly added, "Yet not I, but the grace of God that was with me" (1 Corinthians 15:10). *Paul* worked hard because the *grace of God* worked within him. He said essentially the same thing in Colossians 1:29: "I labor, struggling with all his energy, which so powerfully works in me." In making our real and difficult choices, we depend upon God's empowerment.

We find the greatest example of divine sovereignty and meaningful human choice working together in the crucifixion: "Jesus of Nazareth... was handed over to you by God's set purpose and foreknowledge; and you, with the help of wicked men, put him to death by nailing him to the cross" (Acts 2:22–23).

The early Christians prayed, "Truly in this city there were gathered together against your holy servant Jesus, whom you anointed, both Herod and Pontius Pilate, along with the Gentiles and the peoples of Israel, to do whatever your hand and your plan had predestined to take place" (Acts 4:27–28, ESV). Did Herod and Pilate and the others have sufficient contrary choice to have acted differently to the extent that they could have thwarted the plan God predestined? Clearly not.

While wicked men committed the ultimate evil, God used their freely chosen evil to accomplish ultimate good, so there were two causes for the same event—God and people. But God's cause reigned supreme over the human agency, using it to accomplish his eternal purpose even though the human agents were ignorant of or at odds with that purpose.

> It's consistent to believe in God's sovereignty and yet lock the door.

"The steps of a man are established by the LORD, and He delights in his way" (Psalm 37:23, NASB). The practice of capitalizing pronouns of deity in the NASB and HCSB is helpful here, because it's clear that it is God who delights in the man's choices. So God establishes the man's steps, then when the man makes good choices, God delights in them. The man makes real choices that delight God, but it is God who establishes the man's steps so as to make those good choices possible.

By now, perhaps such thoughts are generating in you a sense of appreciation of God's greatness rather than just another "huh?" Though "huh?" is a natural question, it should prompt us to worship him, not be frustrated that he is so much bigger than we are.

Scripture often portrays God's choices and human choices as intertwined.

I'm using the boxes and lines below as I did in an illustration from D. A. Carson[6] in chapter 5, but given the ground we've covered since then, I want to develop it further, then illustrate how I see it work out in two biblical passages.

Carson explains that the distance from A to B below represents the actions needed to bring about a certain end. One way of viewing this shows God doing more of the work, humans doing less:

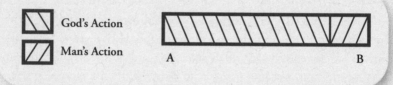

Given Scripture's emphasis on God's sovereignty even in the midst of human choice-making, Carson suggests what Scripture reveals looks something more like this:

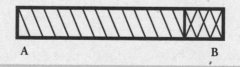

In this scenario, no portion of God's plan—whether large or small—is left *entirely* in the hands of humans. Note that this is not hard determinism; the human being is still there, still choosing, as indicated by his lines. But God is actively at work in human wills to accomplish his sovereign plan even in their part of the partnership.

By "partnership" I mean something in which two beings genuinely participate together, without any implication of equality in intellect, power, or resolve. Any partnership between the infinite Creator God and the finite and currently fallen man is obviously dramatically unequal.

I'll apply this concept to Philippians 2:12–13, ESV:

Man's Action	God's Action
Work out your own salvation with fear and trembling,	
	for it is God who works in you,
	both to will and to work for his good pleasure.

Rather than choosing between the two, Philippians 2:12–13, ESV teaches both, resulting in this:

In other words, we can make this comparison:

Hard determinism teaches ONLY:		—so it's all about God, with man's will nonexistent.
Libertarianism suggests while God's will is vital, God doesn't normally interfere with man's will; it's typically "hands off," which suggests ONLY:		—so believing in and obeying God is mostly about our self-determination and personal effort.

Compatibilism proposes that human choice is real and meaningful, yet *not* "hands off" for God, who works with, empowers, and transforms human wills, which suggests:	▨	—so believing in and obeying God is something he empowers through a work of his Spirit; he calls upon us to genuinely cooperate, which requires effort and discipline, yet we do so by drawing upon his power and grace, not primarily our own self-determination.

Note: Some Arminians would agree with Calvinists concerning what I have labeled as the compatibilist view above and would reject what I have put under the libertarian. This is the difficulty of trying to represent ideas held to by people who genuinely differ in certain beliefs, yet readily agree in others. The important thing isn't the labels; it's the ideas. Call it what you will, I believe it is the third viewpoint above, not the first or second, which best represents the Christian life as depicted in the New Testament.

A similar illustrative breakdown could be made of many other passages, including Colossians 1:29:

Man's Action ◪	God's Action ◩
For this I toil,	
struggling	
	with all his energy

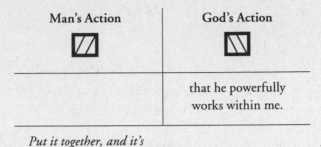

Man's Action	God's Action
	that he powerfully works within me.

Put it together, and it's

God can and does work without human agency. However, he also can and does work in and through human choice, and he can overrule human choice if he so chooses (as he did when he hardened Pharaoh's heart).

God's "Come to me" invitation is genuine.
God invites us and sovereignly empowers us to choose to come to him. His invitation is as real as the possibility of our making a meaningful choice to accept it. Listen:

> Come, all you who are thirsty,
>   come to the waters;
> and you who have no money,
>   come, buy and eat!
> Come, buy wine and milk
>   without money and without cost.
> Why spend money on what is not bread,
>   and your labor on what does not satisfy?
> Listen, listen to me, and eat what is good,
>   and your soul will delight in the richest of fare.
> Give ear and come to me;
>   hear me, that your soul may live. (Isaiah 55:1–3)

Come to me, all you who are weary and burdened, and I will give you rest. (Matthew 11:28)

The Spirit and the bride say, "Come!" And let him who hears say, "Come!" Whoever is thirsty, let him come; and whoever wishes, let him take the free gift of the water of life. (Revelation 22:17)

That final clause is alternatively translated as "whosoever will" (KJV), "let the one who wishes" (NASB), "let the one who desires" (ESV), "let anyone who desires" (NLT), "whoever desires" (HCSB), and "let the one who wants it" (NET). Young's Literal Translation renders the full verse, "And the Spirit and the Bride say, Come; and he who is hearing—let him say, Come; and he who is thirsting—let him come; and he who is willing—let him take the water of life freely."

It's hard to imagine a more sincere invitation. The passage assumes our ability—even if it's a God-given ability (whether through saving grace or prevenient grace)—to make this choice.

Of course, no one verse ever gives the full picture. But I cannot embrace any view of God's sovereignty and human choice that suggests God would use words that lead us to believe meaningful human choice exists when it actually doesn't.

As a young believer I memorized verses printed on small cards sold in Christian bookstores. One of them said, "Him who comes to me I will not cast out" (John 6:37, RSV). I memorized that but didn't bother to look it up in its context (always dangerous). One day I was reading John's gospel and was shocked to see the first part of the verse. Apparently it didn't fit the theology of whoever put together the memory verse cards, since that part got left out: *All that the Father gives me will come to me; and him who comes to me I will not cast out.*

Jesus went on to say, "No one can come to me unless the Father who sent me draws him" (verse 44, ESV). And in case we still don't get the message, he added, "No one can come to me unless it is granted him by the Father" (verse 65). God's drawing and enablement is absolutely necessary for salvation.

My friend Gerry Breshears, a theologian I asked to critique this manuscript, made this comment regarding Christ's statement in John 6:44 that the Father must draw any who will come to him: "However Jesus also says, 'And I, when I am lifted up from the earth, will draw all people to myself' (John 12:32, ESV). If drawing were effectual here, it would make Jesus a universalist. The word translated 'draw' has a range of meaning from 'drag' to 'woo.' It is all who *come* to him, not all who are *drawn,* who will be saved."[7]

"All people" is broad and inclusive. The gospel's larger context makes it clear that not all will be saved; yet when Jesus speaks of dying for the world and drawing all people to himself, he casts his net wide.

Even in the same context, God sometimes gives both sides of the picture. We're not to choose between them but to believe both, even when we don't understand how they fit together.

We freely choose Christ because he empowers us to do so.

We get an intriguing look into this symbiotic process in a passage that has nothing to do with salvation. In 2 Corinthians 8:16–17, the apostle Paul wrote, "I thank God, who put into the heart of Titus the same concern I have for you. For Titus not only welcomed our appeal, but he is coming to you with much enthusiasm and on his own initiative."

God first put a strong love for the Corinthians into Titus's heart, then Titus decided on his own initiative to visit them in Corinth. Apparently, Paul didn't see a contradiction between God's sovereign choice and Titus's meaningful, consequential choice.

It seems that people genuinely respond to God when God first opens their hearts: "One of those listening was a woman named Lydia.... *The Lord opened her heart to respond* to Paul's message" (Acts 16:14).

God calls us spiritually dead without Christ (see Ephesians 2:1). We did not, by acts of our will, make ourselves alive. Rather, "when you were dead in your sins and in the uncircumcision of your sinful nature, *God made you alive with Christ*" (Colossians 2:13).

God extends a genuine—not pretend—invitation to choice-making people to come to him, as he sovereignly empowers them. (From the

Calvinist viewpoint, God empowers only the elect with saving grace, whereas Arminians believe God empowers all people who hear the gospel through prevenient grace—they may or may not respond, but they *can* choose to respond.)

Just as hyper-Calvinists can step outside orthodox Calvinism by denying human choice, hyper-Arminians (a term rarely used) can step outside orthodox Arminianism by believing people have a full capacity, in and of themselves, to respond to God. But this doesn't square with many Scriptures, including John 5:21: "For just as the Father raises the dead and gives them life, even so the Son gives life to whom he is pleased to give it." Here the emphasis is on God's choice.

Notice what Paul wrote about repentance: "Those who oppose him [the Lord's servant] he must gently instruct, in the hope that God will grant them repentance leading them to a knowledge of the truth, and that they will come to their senses and escape from the trap of the devil" (2 Timothy 2:25–26). Sinners should choose to repent, yet only God grants saving repentance. God calls upon us not only to choose to surrender but also to switch sides. We need his empowerment to undergo such a radical transformation of allegiance and identity.

The biblical worldview is not fatalistic; God gives us the command and choice to evangelize the world and to rescue the needy and exploited.

The philosophy of fatalism holds that everything, including evil, suffering, and damnation, happens inevitably, with human beings powerless to effect change. Fatalism predominates among many (not all) Hindus and Muslims. The Arabic term *Insha'Allah* implies that whatever happens is God's will.

Unfortunately, some Christians—hyper-Calvinists, for instance—also reason like fatalists: "If people are elect, God will save them; if they are not, no effort to convert them can bear fruit. Therefore missions and evangelism are senseless."

But Christianized fatalism doesn't end there. I have heard this logic on several occasions, though in language less blunt than my paraphrase: "A sovereign God decrees racism, slavery, and sex trafficking; they exist, and his will cannot be thwarted, therefore they are his will—so why should we battle them? To do so would be to fight against God."

I've been told by several evangelical pastors that we should accept abortion as God's way of populating Heaven, since if those aborted babies were allowed to live, most of them would never be saved.

In contrast, the Bible calls upon people to choose to take action, speak up for, and help the poor and needy (see, for example, Proverbs 31:8–9 and James 1:27). This is the polar opposite of fatalism.

Albert Einstein said, "The world is too dangerous to live in—not because of people who do evil, but because of people who sit and let it happen."[8] Some of that stems from indifference, some from fatalism.

Since God can use even evil for his glory, if I try to stop a sin, am I in danger of trying to thwart God's will? No, because God commands us to intervene to stop injustice, so that his moral will can be done.

Scripture teaches that humans make real choices and that we must resist evil, yet God remains sovereign in a nonfatalistic way. He offers us choices and encourages us to pray that he bring about changes, and to do what we can to change our lives and the world itself. God uses the proclamation of his Word to save the lost (see Romans 10:14–15). Paul says, "We are ambassadors for Christ, as though God were making an appeal through us; we beg you on behalf of Christ, be reconciled to God" (2 Corinthians 5:20).

This is not the language of icy predetermination that supposes God has no passion to reach the lost, or that human beings have no role in his plan to do so. Any theological position that prompts us to think otherwise is foreign to God's Word and to the original followers of Jesus.

Some professing compatibilists talk like hyper-Calvinists. They minimize human choice, as if it were invented by Arminians rather than God. Isn't it disingenuous for a compatibilist to imply that God's sovereign determination negates rather than embraces meaningful human choice? Why does God reward those who help the poor and share the gospel, and hold accountable those who don't? Doesn't it glorify God more to see him as sovereign over a universe full of choice-making creatures than as a puppeteer?

Scripture shows God's hand at work in a broken world.

The Bible consistently ascribes to God the problem of infertility. It's said of Hannah, "The LORD had closed her womb" (1 Samuel 1:5). Sarah said, "The LORD has kept me from having children" (Genesis 16:2). God opened Leah's womb (see Genesis 29:31). Samson's mother and John the Baptist's mother both had children by God's intervention (see Judges 13:3; Luke 1:13). God oversees the conception of children and works directly to shape the child: "[God] knit me together in my mother's womb" (Psalm 139:13).

God chooses our financial situation. First Samuel 2:7–8 says, "The LORD sends poverty and wealth; he humbles and he exalts. He raises the poor from the dust and lifts the needy from the ash heap."

God grants limited and conditional power to people, but he, the power dispenser, still maintains control. Pilate was the most powerful person in Jerusalem. He wanted Jesus to acknowledge this, asking him, "Do you not know that I have authority to release you and authority to crucify you?" (John 19:10, ESV). Unimpressed, Jesus answered him, "You would have no authority over me at all unless it had been given you from above" (verse 11, ESV).

God determines the times and places of people and nations. Acts 17:25–26 says God "gives all men life and breath and everything else" and that "from one man he made every nation of men, that they should inhabit the whole earth; and he determined the times set for them and the exact places where they should live."

What is problematic to us is no problem to God.

Prayerful examination of the deep questions of God's sovereignty and our choices ought to humble us, especially when it seems mysterious and we can't see how everything fits together.

Edwin Abbott's novel *Flatland* concerns a world in which there are only two dimensions, length and breadth. There's no depth. Eventually the narrator, a square, is visited by a three-dimensional sphere. Square cannot comprehend the third dimension until he's taken to Spaceland to see it.

Astronomer Hugh Ross used a similar analogy concerning our difficulty understanding certain aspects of God's Word.[9] While we live in four dimensions (length, breadth, depth, and time), God exists outside of both time and space, so he has reference points we can't even imagine. Consequently, the coexistence of such doctrines as election and predestination, or sovereignty and free will—which to us can seem impossible (or at least logically absurd) because of our restricted frames of reference—is fully obvious to him. (What *isn't* obvious to God?)

Theories dealing with God's choices and ours have apparently insurmountable problems—not because we're so logical, but because we're finite and therefore our logic is finite. Consider the argument that if God knows you're going to buy at 3:09 p.m. tomorrow that mocha I mentioned earlier, then when the time comes you have no real choice. But suppose God exists not in one dimension of time but three. Hugh Ross states, "A three-dimensional time domain or its equivalent would enable God to predetermine every action of every human being while sustaining the operation of human choice."[10]

You don't have to agree with that conclusion to get the point that we're extremely limited in our thinking.

On the next page I've attempted to illustrate our dilemma using two straight lines indicating God's sovereignty and human choice. They don't appear to touch each other, so they're depicted as parallel lines that don't intersect—or if they do, it's outside of our vision.

We can't imagine how these two things are compatible. Sure, God could have choices and we could have choices, but how could God's choices be sovereign if we can oppose and violate them? This can frustrate us—or it can impart awe and wonder as we ponder a God who has the ability to see things with absolute understanding and to accomplish them with infinite power.

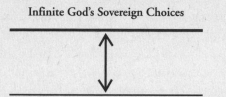

Our Perspective

Infinite God's Sovereign Choices

No Clear Connection:
Paradox, Mystery

Finite Creatures' Choices

God sees multi-dimensionally. When he looks at what puzzles our brains with our flatland perspective, he may see something more like this:

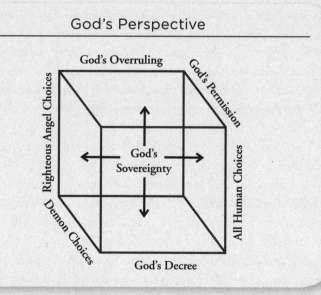

God's Perspective

God's Overruling

God's Permission

Righteous Angel Choices

God's
Sovereignty

All Human Choices

Demon Choices

God's Decree

As suggested in the six sides of this cube, God and his view of complete reality is much bigger than ours. (Of course, in reality, his view is *infinitely* bigger, and three dimensions aren't nearly enough; I'm not trying to put God in a box but to take him out of the one we often put him in.) God sees forces constantly at work that we're unaware of. He simultaneously sees and deals with all human choices and all demon choices, including Satan's. He sees and deals with the choices of righteous angels. He makes choices himself, decrees creatures' choices, permits creatures' choices, and overrules their choices if he so wishes.

This may make our heads spin, but it's no challenge for God. He sees and works in other dimensions we don't even comprehend. While we stare at those two lines wondering how they might intersect, he deals with countless billions of intersections of that which he decrees and permits related to the choices of his creatures, while he governs every detail of the physical universe in which we live, which is something like a hundred billion light years in expanse.

> God sees and works in other dimensions
> we don't even comprehend.

God reveals seemingly inscrutable or irreconcilable truths, which may confuse us but make perfect sense to him. We should trust what he says, and let the greatness and beauty of his truth—too big for us to comprehend—prompt us to praise and worship him.

God's sovereignty and human choice are an unequal partnership, not a competition.

Archibald Alexander, advocating the compatibilist perspective, claimed, "Calvinism is the broadest of systems. It regards the divine sovereignty and the freedom of the human will as the two sides of a roof which come together as a ridgepole above the clouds. Calvinism accepts both truths. A system which denies either one of the two has only half a roof over its head."[11]

While I doubt anyone this side of Heaven will ever manage to fully "explain" how God's sovereignty and human choice fully fit together, I believe Scripture provides us with many examples of how the two work symbiotically.

For example, Paul called himself not only a "servant" of God but also a "fellow worker" with God (1 Corinthians 3:9; see also Titus 1:1). While Paul never lost sight of God's sovereignty, he also recognized himself as God's partner in the work of the gospel (see 2 Corinthians 6:1; see also 1 Peter 4:13). These are the kinds of passages that emboldened me to title this book *hand in Hand.*

Paul made his evangelistic plans (see Romans 1:13; 15:24; 2 Corinthians 1:15–17), often in line with his personal preference for pioneering work (see Romans 15:20). And yet he held those plans loosely, always submitting them to God's sovereign plan (see Acts 16:1–10). In this way, both Paul and God made choices that altered world history.

When the prophet Elisha lay dying, King Jehoash of Israel came to see him. The meeting took place at a time when the people of Aram were severely "oppressing" the Israelites. Without explaining himself, Elisha instructed the king to take some arrows out of his quiver and strike the ground with them. The king obeyed, but feebly; he stopped after just three strikes. The angry prophet responded, "You should have struck the ground five or six times; then you would have defeated Aram and completely destroyed it. But now you will defeat it only three times" (2 Kings 13:18–19). Jehoash's halfhearted choice meant the difference between temporary victory and total triumph—a *very* consequential difference.

Consider Daniel's long prayer of confession (see Daniel 9:4–19). He'd read the book of Jeremiah and saw that the seventy years prophesied for Israel's exile had almost come to an end. Had some of us been in Daniel's place, we would have exclaimed, "Bring it on, Lord!" But not Daniel. He got down on his knees and prayed one of the Bible's longest prayers, asking God to restore Israel to her land—exactly what God said he would do.

It seems that Daniel had a different idea of "sovereignty" than many of us do. All too often, those ideas make us passive, but they launched Daniel into a fervent period of activity and focused prayer.

Would Daniel have received the remarkable prophecy of verses 20–27 if he hadn't prayed the remarkable prayer of verses 4–19? (We're told in verse 23 that God dispatched Gabriel, his messenger angel, only after Daniel started praying.) Did God's response to Daniel's prayer constitute a change in the way God fulfilled Jeremiah's prophecy? Who knows?

When I think of the examples of Paul, Elisha, and Daniel, I can't help but marvel at the beauty of the unequal but real partnerships forged when we submit our choices to God and walk hand in Hand—his the strong and sovereign Hand lovingly reaching down, ours the weak hand eagerly reaching up.

Notes

The second epigraph is from Ken Hensley, interview by Dmitry M. Epstein, "Interview with Ken Hensley," Let It Rock, November 2004, http://dmme.net/interviews/hensley3.html.

1. A. W. Tozer, *The Knowledge of the Holy* (San Francisco, CA: HarperOne, 1992), 174.

2. G. I. Williamson, *The Westminster Confession of Faith* (Phillipsburg, NJ: P & R Publishing, 2003), 39.

3. D. A. Carson, *Divine Sovereignty and Human Responsibility: Biblical Perspective in Tension* (Eugene, OR: Wipf and Stock, 2002), 24–35.

4. Carson, *Divine Sovereignty and Human Responsibility,* 18.

5. Carl Sagan, *The Demon-Haunted World: Science as a Candle* (New York: Ballantine Books, 1996), 9.

6. Carson, *Divine Sovereignty and Human Responsibility,* 211.

7. Gerry Breshears, comment in manuscript critique, May 24, 2014.

8. Dean L. Overman, *A Case for the Existence of God* (Lanham, MD: Rowman and Littlefield, 2009), 99.

9. Hugh Ross, *Beyond the Cosmos: What Recent Discoveries in Astrophysics Reveal About the Glory and Love of God* (Colorado Springs, CO: NavPress, 1996), 52–53.

10. Ross, *Beyond the Cosmos,* 162.

11. A. H. Strong, *Systematic Theology* (Philadelphia: American Baptist Publication Society, 1907), 1:364.

Voices from the Past Share Timeless Truths

We can make a large horse go wherever we want by means of a small bit in its mouth.... If you are wise and understand God's ways, prove it by living an honorable life, doing good works with the humility that comes from wisdom.

James 3:3, 13, NLT

These two truths, God's Sovereignty and Man's Responsibility, are to be believed firmly, held tenaciously, proclaimed fully, and our life is to be lived in the light thereof.

W. H. Griffith Thomas

Modern believers have a bad habit of acting as if the Christian faith began with us, with the result that we end up doing "theology on the fly," ignoring a few thousand years of Christian history as if not much of importance was learned.

We tend to think that what's trending on Twitter is somehow important just because it's current, when the fact that it's popular and fashionable in all probability means it's decidedly unimportant. We tend to be guilty of what C. S. Lewis called "chronological snobbery," the flawed belief that newer ideas are always better than old ones. There's a lot of trendy theology these days; like puffs of smoke on a windy day, most of it won't last, and shouldn't.

When it comes to sovereignty and free will, it's a fair assumption that the best thinking has already been done. That's why in this book, and especially in this chapter, I cite a lot of "dead people" whose wisdom has passed the test of time, and who are very much alive in the presence of Christ. It excites me to consider that we who love Jesus will have the opportunity to speak with these brilliant people, after the resurrection, at dinner parties on the New Earth. Perhaps we'll discuss some of the very issues in this book, but with a great deal more insight—especially with Jesus there to respond to our questions!

Throughout history, Calvinists and Arminians have weighed in, often disagreeing but sometimes agreeing more than we suppose. A. H. Strong, a four-point Calvinist, said in his *Systematic Theology*, "The man who carries a vase of gold-fish does not prevent the fish from moving unrestrainedly within the vase."[1]

Samuel Fisk developed this analogy further:

> He may determine, unhindered, whether he will place the bowl
> on the table, on the window sill, or on the piano; near the light
> or in the shade; etc. If he is benevolent we may suppose that he
> will so act as to insure the best conditions for the goldfish. And
> his will is overruling. The fish themselves, however, within the
> well-defined limits of their bowl, have a measure of free choice.
> They may swim one way or another, or they may cease from all
> swimming and rest on the bottom of the bowl or float near the
> top of the water. As food is available, they may partake of little or
> much or none at all. The superior creature, man, does not force
> the food down their throats nor determine the exact amount
> which each individual fish will partake of.[2]

Alexander Maclaren, who makes nearly every short list of great Calvinist preachers, said words it's hard to imagine any Arminian disagreeing with:

> Obedience is in our power to give or to withhold.... God's grace constrains no man, and there is always the possibility open that when He calls we refuse, and that when He beseeches we say, "I will not."... But the practical point that I have to urge is this: There are two mysteries, the one that men can, and the other that men do, resist Christ's pleading voice.... If I cannot trust my sense that I can do this thing or not do it, as I choose, there is nothing that I can trust. Will is the power of determining which of two roads I shall go.... God, the infinite Will, has given to men, whom He made in His own image, this inexplicable and awful power of coinciding with or opposing His purposes and His voice.[3]

On the other hand, the human condition is such that people are spiritually helpless without God. A. W. Pink used this illustration to explain his Calvinist viewpoint:

> I hold in my hand a book. I release it; what happens? It falls. In which direction? Downwards; always downwards. Why? Because, answering the law of gravity, its own weight sinks it. Suppose I desire that book to occupy a position three feet higher; then what? I must lift it; a power outside of that book must raise it. Such is the relationship which fallen man sustains toward God. Whilst Divine power upholds him, he is preserved from plunging still deeper into sin; let that power be withdrawn, and he falls—his own weight (of sin) drags him down. God does not push him down, any more than I did that book.[4]

Pink goes on to say what most Calvinists and some Arminians would agree with: "How then is the sinner to move heavenwards? By an act of his own will? Not so. A power outside of himself must grasp hold of him and lift him every inch of the way."[5]

On the one hand, since Arminians believe in prevenient grace—that God must extend himself to empower a sinner to believe—they should at least partly agree with Pink. But some Arminians might struggle with the notion that God must "lift him every inch of the way." They might prefer only *some* or *most* of the way. If, however, they agree that God must grab hold of them and lift them every inch of the way, then they are embracing a doctrine their Calvinist friends hold dear.

Charles Spurgeon demonstrated the importance of consistency with Scripture over consistency with one's preferred theological leanings.

Spurgeon advised, "Brethren be willing to see both sides of the shield of truth. Rise above the babyhood which cannot believe two doctrines until it sees the connecting link. Have you not two eyes, man? Must you needs put one of them out in order to see clearly?"[6]

I think Spurgeon comes as close as anyone I've read to articulating what Scripture as a whole reveals. Sadly, I never read Spurgeon in Bible college and seminary. I'd been a pastor for ten years before I discovered him, and then I couldn't get enough of him. The Bible oozed out of his pores, and he let Scripture be Scripture, rarely twisting it to fit his theology.

Spurgeon maintained that no man-made theological system is authoritative. He said, "My love of consistency with my own doctrinal views is not great enough to allow me knowingly to alter a single text of Scripture. I have great respect for orthodoxy, but my reverence for inspiration is far greater. I would sooner a hundred times over appear to be inconsistent with myself than be inconsistent with the word of God."[7]

While the Bible is God breathed, theological systems are not. They are valid *not* to the extent that they're self-consistent but to the degree they're consistent with Scripture.

Spurgeon didn't try to reconcile the paradoxical doctrines we've considered. It's worth repeating in its larger context a sentence of his I cited earlier: "That God predestines, and that man is responsible, are two things that few can see. They are believed to be inconsistent and contradictory; but they are not. It is just the fault of our weak judgment. Two truths cannot be contradictory to each other.…These two truths, I do not believe, can ever be welded into one upon any human anvil, but one they shall be in eternity."[8]

He warned against attempting to solve, by means of shortsighted logic, every apparent biblical problem: "Men who are morbidly anxious to possess a self-consistent creed,—a creed which they can put together, and form into a square, like a Chinese puzzle,—are very apt to narrow their souls.… Those who will only believe what they can reconcile will necessarily disbelieve much of Divine revelation."[9]

> While the Bible is God breathed, theological systems are not.

Spurgeon never apologized for his Calvinism, but first and foremost he was about following Jesus and God's Word. He said, "I wish to be called nothing but a Christian; but if you ask me, do I hold the doctrinal views which were held by John Calvin, I reply, I do in the main hold them, and rejoice to avow it."[10]

We should be passionate about the whole truth, not just part of it. A. W. Tozer spoke insightfully of sovereignty and meaningful human choice:

> God sovereignly decreed that man should be free to exercise moral choice, and man from the beginning has fulfilled that decree by making his choice between good and evil. When he chooses to do evil, he does not thereby countervail the sovereign will of God but fulfills it, inasmuch as the eternal decree decided not which choice

the man should make but that he should be free to make it. If in His absolute freedom God has willed to give man limited freedom, who is there to stay His hand.... Man's will is free because God is sovereign.[11]

Often we turn our lack of understanding into a reason not to believe, or pursue a misguided attempt to make sense of everything by forcing Scripture's square pegs into the round holes of our brains. In the process we squeeze Scripture into our own mold and read into the Bible selectively, to make it fit with what we've been taught or want to believe.

Charles Simeon (1758–1836) reinvigorated the English church with his emphasis on the primacy of Scripture and the necessity of practical application.

Simeon was a Calvinist but disliked the label. In a sermon on Romans 9:16, he said,

Many there are who cannot see these truths [the doctrines of God's sovereignty], who yet are in a state truly pleasing to God; yea many, at whose feet the best of us may be glad to be found in heaven. It is a great evil, when these doctrines are made a ground of separation one from another, and when the advocates of different systems anathematize each other.... Mutual kindness and concession are far better than vehement argumentation and uncharitable discussion.[12]

Simeon practiced what he preached. We get a glimpse of this through a conversation he had with John Wesley, reported by Simeon himself.

"Sir," Simeon said to Wesley, "I understand that you are called an Arminian; and I have been sometimes called a Calvinist; and therefore I suppose we are to draw daggers. But before I consent to begin the combat, with your permission I will ask you a few questions.... Pray, Sir, do you feel yourself a depraved creature, so depraved that you would never have thought of turning unto God, if God had not first put it into your heart?"

"Yes," answered Wesley, "I do indeed."

"And do you utterly despair of recommending yourself to God by anything that you can do," Simeon continued, "and look for salvation solely through the blood and righteousness of Christ?"

"Yes, solely through Christ," Wesley replied.

"But, Sir, supposing you were at first saved by Christ, are you not somehow or other to save yourself afterwards by your own works?"

"No; I must be saved by Christ from first to last."

"Allowing, then, that you were first turned by the grace of God, are you not in some way or other to keep yourself by your own power?"

"No."

"What then, are you to be upheld every hour and every moment by God, as much as an infant in its mother's arms?"

"Yes; altogether."

"And is all your hope in the grace and mercy of God to preserve you unto his heavenly kingdom?"

"Yes; I have no hope, but in him."

"Then, Sir, with your leave, I will put up my dagger again; for this is all my Calvinism; this is my election, my justification by faith, my final perseverance: it is, in substance, all that I hold, and as I hold it: and therefore, if you please, instead of searching out terms and phrases to be a ground of contention between us, we will cordially unite in those things wherein we agree."[13]

> I admire the spirit of anyone who starts by looking for common ground; sometimes you'll find a great deal more than you expect.

Of course, the Wesley and Simeon story doesn't mean Calvinism and Arminianism are the same. They aren't. Some Arminians would give different answers than Wesley did, and some Calvinists would ask different questions than Simeon. But I admire the spirit of anyone who starts by looking for common ground; sometimes you'll find a great deal more than you expect.

Charles Simeon set a great example of putting Scripture above theological systems.

James Houston said of Simeon,

> He never believed one theological system had a monopoly on truth.... Instead, Simeon sought to "give every text its just meaning, its natural bearing, and its legitimate use." He urged his hearers not to be sectarian, but to cultivate a devout and ecumenical spirit that focused upon the authority of the Bible in daily living. His aim was to make "Bible Christians" out of his hearers so that they lived out the reality of the gospel as revealed in the Holy Scriptures.[14]

John Stott wrote that Simeon lived in a period when the controversy between "Calvinists" and "Arminians" was heated, even bitter. Yet...he wrote:

> The author is...no friend to systematizers in theology. He has endeavored to derive from the Scriptures alone his views of religion; never wresting any portion of the Word of God to favor a particular opinion, but giving to every part of it that sense, which it seems to him to have been designed by its great Author to convey.[15]

What Simeon feared, Stott wrote, "was the development of a complete and rigid system; for then, when new light breaks forth from the Word, the systematizer is faced with the painful dilemma of either adapting his system to absorb the freshly perceived truth or of trimming the truth to fit his system. The latter is the temptation of tidy minds."[16]

(This wasn't a condemnation of systematic theology per se, a discipline I greatly value. Rather, Simeon's concern was that the compulsion to systematize sometimes pushes people to close their eyes to some biblical truths while locking them exclusively on others.)

Simeon wrote to a friend in 1825, "Sometimes I am a high Calvinist, at other times a low Arminian, so that if extremes will please you, I am your man; only remember, it is not *one* extreme that we are to go to, but *both* extremes."[17]

There are other doctrines besides sovereignty and free will that we must hold in balance.

The humanity and deity of Christ is one among many examples. The early Christ-followers faced a number of heretical teachings. Docetism affirmed Christ's deity while denying his humanity. Ebionism affirmed his humanity but denied his deity. Nestorianism said that Christ's deity and humanity were two separate natures rather than one unified nature. Each of these heresies was the result of failing to simultaneously embrace two biblical teachings that are hard to reconcile. In fact, most doctrinal heresies are misguided attempts to push an orthodox position to its logical conclusions while failing to affirm with equal vigor a corresponding but apparently contradictory biblical teaching. In the arena of sovereignty and free will, this accounts for the heretical extremes of hyper-Calvinism and open theism. The first takes sovereignty to its logical conclusions with no regard for the biblical teaching about human choice; the second takes free will to its logical conclusions at the expense of God's sovereignty as well as his omniscience.

Simeon wrote, "When I come to a text which speaks of election, I delight myself in the doctrine of election. When the Apostles exhort me to repentance and obedience, and indicate my freedom of choice and action, I give myself up to that side of the question."[18]

This is where we need to remind ourselves of both mystery and beauty. Simeon said, "As wheels in a complicated machine may move in opposite directions and yet subserve one common end, so may truths *apparently opposite* be perfectly reconcilable with each other, and equally subserve the purposes of God in the accomplishment of man's salvation."[19]

The best theological label is "Berean."

When Emerson wrote "A foolish consistency is the hobgoblin of little minds,"[20] he was challenging us to accept truth even when it requires expanding our minds and breaking from our tidy little systems. Good words for Bible students.

William Symington wrote, "Our object should not be to have Scripture on our side but to be on the side of Scripture; and however dear any sentiment may have become by being long entertained, so soon as it is seen to be contrary to the Bible, we must be prepared to abandon it without hesitation."[21] Our allegiance to a particular theological system can hinder this process.

> We shouldn't search the writings of Wesley or Calvin to examine whether a teaching is true; we should search the Scriptures.

The Berean Christians were commended for carefully examining, in light of the Scriptures, the teachings of the apostle Paul (see Acts 17:11). This is a man who eventually wrote thirteen inspired biblical books. How much more should we evaluate the teachings of everyone else we read or listen to!

We can benefit greatly from the work of Bible scholars and authors. I certainly have. But we shouldn't search the writings of Calvin or Wesley to examine whether a teaching is true; we should search the Scriptures.

I mentioned earlier that it was in an Arminian church where I, as a teenager, found God (though now I think of it more as him finding me). Imagine a one-to-ten continuum in which one represents pure Arminianism and ten is pure Calvinism. (I'm speaking now only of the orthodox versions of each.) On that scale, I began at around two and have since settled at around eight.

I attended Multnomah Bible College and Western Seminary. Each had faculty members from across the Arminian-Calvinist spectrum. The professor who influenced my approach to reading Scripture more than any other was not a Bible or theology teacher. It was Ed Goodrich, my Greek prof at Multnomah, who often told us, as we translated the entire New Testament over the course of three years, "Better to be at home with your Bible and not your theology, than to be at home with your theology and not your Bible." Time and again we would grapple with the proper translation and meaning of texts—the temptation was always to see the text in light of the doctrine we'd been taught rather than letting the text change our doctrinal views.

I love studying theology. But if the Bible never challenges us to re-think our theology, it's because our theology, not our Bible, is our author-ity. We should seek to change that.

We can continue the discussion together in Heaven.

On the subject of showing respect for brothers and sisters in Christ of different traditions, Emo Phillips tells a story with more truth in it than there ought to be:

> I was walking across a bridge one day, and I saw a man standing on the edge, about to jump off. So I ran over and said "Stop! Don't do it!" "Why shouldn't I?" he said. I said, "Well, there's so much to live for!" He said, "Like what?" I said, "Well...are you religious or atheist?" He said, "Religious." I said, "Me too! Are you Christian or Buddhist?" He said, "Christian." I said, "Me too! Are you Catholic or Protestant?" He said, "Protestant." I said, "Me too! Are you Episcopalian or Baptist?" He said, "Baptist!" I said, "Wow! Me too! Are you Baptist church of God or Baptist church of the Lord?" He said, "Baptist church of God!" I said, "Me too! Are you original Baptist church of God, or are you reformed Baptist church of God?" He said, "Reformed Baptist church of God!" I said, "Me too! Are you reformed Baptist church of God, reformation of 1879, or reformed Baptist church of God, reformation of 1915?" He said, "Reformed Baptist church of God, reformation of 1915!" I said, "Die, heretic scum," and pushed him off.[22]

Contrast this with what Arminius said about Calvin:

> After the reading of Scripture, which I strenuously inculcate, and more than any other...I recommend that the Commentaries of Calvin be read.... For I affirm that in the interpretation of the Scriptures Calvin is incomparable, and that his Commentaries are more to be valued than anything that is handed down to us in the Bibliotheca [writings] of the Fathers; so much so, that I concede to him a certain spirit of prophecy [interpretation] in which he stands distinguished above others, above most, yea above all.... But here I add—with discrimination; as the writings of all men ought to be read.[23]

It's hard to imagine Arminius so enthusiastically recommending Calvin's commentaries unless he agreed with the great majority of what they said. That itself is remarkable, and should challenge modern Arminians and Calvinists to drop the assumption that we disagree on most issues. In fact we disagree on *some,* and it would be healthy to remind ourselves of the many things about which we agree.

I'm thankful too for the example of John Wesley, who said, "John Calvin was a pious, learned, sensible man; and so was [Jacobus Arminius]. Many Calvinists are pious, learned, sensible men; and so are many Arminians."

Wesley went on to ask, "Is it not the duty of every Arminian preacher, First, never, in public or in private, to use the word *Calvinist* as a term of reproach; seeing it is neither better nor worse than calling names?—a practice no more consistent with good sense or good manners, than it is with Christianity. Secondly, to do all that in him lies to prevent his hearers from doing it, by showing them the sin and folly of it?"[24]

Both John Calvin and John Wesley were intelligent, compassionate, clear-thinking Biblicists, unworthy of name-calling or dismissal. Unfortunately, in my experience, Arminians rarely think of Calvinists as compassionate, and Calvinists rarely think of Arminians as clear thinking.

Although John Wesley and George Whitefield became close friends while studying at Oxford University, theological differences eventually brought them into sharp conflict. Wesley became known for his Arminianism and Whitefield for his Calvinism.

Later the two reconciled; before Whitefield died, he requested that Wesley preach at three memorial services to be held for him in London. These are the historical facts, but a fascinating story circulates to this day that, if true, puts an exclamation point on the debate. (I say "if true" because the story survives in enough different versions to suggest it could be apocryphal. But if it isn't true, it should have been!)

The most common version of the tale has a woman approaching Wesley after Whitefield's death to ask, "Mr. Wesley, do you expect to see dear Mr. Whitefield in Heaven?" Wesley supposedly paused for some time before replying with great seriousness, "No, madam."

The woman, who loved and admired both men, replied sadly, "I was afraid you would say so."

"Do not misunderstand me, madam," Wesley continued. "George Whitefield was so bright a star in the firmament of God's glory, and will stand so near the throne, that one like me, who am less than the least, will never catch a glimpse of him."

When I meet Wesley and Whitefield in Heaven, I hope I'll discover the story to be true, but I know I'll find two dear friends, united in the love of Jesus, both having had to make a few theological adjustments, as will I. Meanwhile, I want the same gracious spirit to characterize my own approach to these issues.

I do know that John Wesley said this at Whitefield's death: "There are many doctrines of a less essential nature, with regard to which, even the most sincere children of God…are and have been divided for many ages. In these we may think and let think; we may 'agree to disagree.'"[25]

Spurgeon, as a Calvinist, showed his own respect for John Wesley:

If there were wanted two apostles to be added to the number of the twelve, I do not believe that there could be found two men more fit to be so added than George Whitefield and John Wesley. The character of John Wesley stands beyond all imputation for self-sacrifice, zeal, holiness, and communion with God; he lived far above the ordinary level of common Christians, and was one "of whom the world was not worthy." I believe there are multitudes of men who cannot see these truths, or, at least, cannot see them in the way in which we put them, who nevertheless have received Christ as their Saviour, and are as dear to the heart of the God of grace as the soundest Calvinist in or out of Heaven.[26]

Notes

The second epigraph is from Dr. W. H. Griffith Thomas, *St. Paul's Epistle to the Romans: A Devotional Commentary* (Grand Rapids, MI: Eerdmans, 1946), 266.

1. A. H. Strong, *Systematic Theology* (Philadelphia: The Griffith & Rowland Press, 1907), 363.

2. Samuel Fisk, *Divine Sovereignty and Human Freedom: Seeing Both Sides* (Neptune, NJ: Loizeaux Brothers, 1973), 58.

3. Alexander Maclaren, quoted in Samuel Fisk, *Election and Predestination: Keys to a Clearer Understanding* (Eugene, OR: Wipf and Stock, 1997), 14.

4. A. W. Pink, *The Sovereignty of God* (Mulberry, IN: Sovereign Grace, 2008), 168.

5. Pink, *The Sovereignty of God,* 168.

6. C. H. Spurgeon, "Faith and Regeneration" (sermon 979, March 5, 1871, Metropolitan Tabernacle, Newington), www.spurgeon.org/sermons/0979.htm.

7. C. H. Spurgeon, "Salvation by Knowing the Truth" (sermon 1516, January 16, 1880, Metropolitan Tabernacle, Newington), www.spurgeon.org/sermons/1516.htm.

8. C. H. Spurgeon, "Sovereign Grace and Man's Responsibility" (sermon 207, Royal Surrey Gardens, August 1, 1858), www.spurgeon.org/sermons/0207.htm.

9. C. H. Spurgeon, "Faith," in *An All-Round Ministry: Addresses to Ministers and Students,* www.spurgeon.org/misc/aarm01.htm.

10. C. H. Spurgeon, *The Autobiography of Charles H. Spurgeon,* 1834–1854, comp. Susannah Spurgeon and Joseph Harrald (Chicago: Fleming H. Revell, 1898), 1:176.

11. A. W. Tozer, *The Knowledge of the Holy* (San Francisco, CA: HarperOne, 1992), 121–22.

12. Charles Simeon, *Horae Homileticae: Romans* (London: Holdsworth and Ball, 1833), 15:357.

13. Simeon, *Horae Homileticae: Genesis to Leviticus,* 1:xvii–xviii.

14. James M. Houston in Charles Simeon, *Evangelical Preaching: An Anthology of Sermons by Charles Simeon,* ed. James M. Houston and John R. W. Stott (Vancouver, BC: Regent College Publishing, 2003), xxiii.

15. John R. W. Stott in Charles Simeon, *Evangelical Preaching,* 4–5.

16. John R. W. Stott in Charles Simeon, *Evangelical Preaching,* 5.

17. Handley Carr Glyn Moule, *English Leaders of Religion: Charles Simeon* (London: Methuen, 1892), 97–98.

18. Charles Simeon, *Memoirs of the Life of the Rev. Charles Simeon, M.A.,* ed. William Carus (London: Hatchard and Son, 1847), 674.

19. Simeon, *Horae Homileticae: Genesis to Leviticus,* 1:xxiii.

20. Ralph Waldo Emerson, *The Essay on Self-Reliance* (East Aurora, NY: Roycrofters, 1908), 23.

21. Roy Blackwood, *William Symington: Penman of the Scottish Covenanters* (Grand Rapids, MI: Reformation Heritage Books, 2009), n. p.

22. Emo Phillips, quoted in Lee Cozar, "The Wisdom of Emo Phillips," http://cmgm.stanford.edu/~lkozar/EmoPhillips.html.

23. Caspar Brandt, *The Life of James Arminius, D.D.,* trans. John Guthrie (London: Ward, 1854), 235–36.

24. John Wesley, *The Works of the Reverend John Wesley, A. M.,* ed. John Emory (New York: J. Collord, 1831), 6:134 (with grammatical correction).

25. Wesley, *Works,* 1:477.

26. C. H. Spurgeon, *Autobiography,* 1:176.

Trusting God to Weave All Choices Together for His Children's Good

Now do not be distressed or angry with yourselves because you sold me here, for God sent me before you to preserve life.

Genesis 45:5, ESV

God in His love always wills what is best for us. In His wisdom He always knows what is best, and in His sovereignty He has the power to bring it about.

Jerry Bridges

A dear friend of ours was raped. I can't begin to imagine the pain she has suffered, yet she believes God had a purpose for allowing this terrible evil. Even though she was unable to raise the baby conceived through her rape, she knows the child has an appointed future in a loving home.

The man who raped her was not caught, but he will not get away with his crime: "It is a fearful thing to fall into the hands of the living God" (Hebrews 10:31, ESV).

Our friend chose not to allow the act of an evil man to dictate her future but instead chooses to trust the plan of almighty God, who created her and went to the cross for her—and for her child. And though the words don't come easily and could be misunderstood, I say this with conviction: God never ceased to watch over her and love her the day the rapist attacked her.

God can and does use evil to bring about good.

Our fates do not rest in the hands of fallen humankind: politicians, lawyers, military officers, employers, or even spouses and children. No matter what happens, and how much it hurts, God is fully capable of using painful events for good.

It is not inconsistent or unjust of him to utilize the low-purposed, finite evil of men and demons for his high-purposed, infinite good. This reality should prompt us to worship him for his greatness and his ability to use even what displeases him to accomplish what will ultimately please both him and us.

> No matter what happens, and how much it hurts, God is fully capable of using painful events for good.

God can use even evil spirits to accomplish his purposes.

Critics who argue that the Bible contradicts itself sometimes cite pairs of passages such as 2 Samuel 24:1 and 1 Chronicles 21:1 to prove their point. The first verse says God incited David to take a census of Israel, while the second says Satan prompted David's decision. Which is correct?

Both.

Three times Scripture says God sent evil spirits: once to judge a murderer (see Judges 9:23–24), once to torment King Saul (see 1 Samuel 16:14–23), and once to deceive evil King Ahab (see 1 Kings 22:19–23). Some argue these are demons, others that they're human spirits.

The Bible also tells us of some rebellious people to whom God sends "a powerful delusion," in a context speaking about the work of Satan (2 Thessalonians 2:11–12).

God is not guilty of evil, but as Creator he still uses his creatures, including demons, to bring judgment on evil people. I would never have come up with such an idea on my own. I wouldn't believe it, except for the fact that God's Word reveals it, and therefore I adjust my theology accordingly.

God can use evil without committing it.

Some imagine that God's use of evil means that he commits it, approves of it, or fails to judge it. They are categorically wrong.

God remained sovereign when our friend was raped, but I believe his fierce anger erupted at the evil done to his precious daughter. I believe this because of what the Bible says: "Be sure of this: The wicked will not go unpunished, but those who are righteous will go free" (Proverbs 11:21).

Some claim that affirming God's sovereign grace in the context of human evil justifies evildoing. Paul refuted such thinking:

Someone might argue, "If my falsehood enhances God's truthfulness and so increases his glory, why am I still condemned as a sinner?" Why not say—as we are being slanderously reported as saying and as some claim that we say—"Let us do evil that good may result"? Their condemnation is deserved. (Romans 3:7–8)

God's sovereign ability to use evil doesn't justify or minimize evildoing; it simply shows that he's infinitely superior to any evildoer and that his plan to do good to his people will not be derailed by any creature.

It's true that God hated the crime committed against our friend. It stirred his great wrath. It's also true that he could have stopped the rape and prevented much heartache. Yet, if Romans 8:28—the promise that he'll work all things together for her good—applies to the great groan-causing suffering mentioned in that verse's immediate context, then it surely applies to hers also. It would be terribly insensitive to say this, were it not God's revealed truth. And it gives hope where there is none.

Because God permits evils with deliberate purpose, in line with his bringing eternal blessing, then even though we don't understand how, he deserves our trust.

God is both omnipotent and wise.

We are puzzled sometimes because God could have shown his power by preventing tragedies and healing diseases, but chose not to. We would prefer that God crush evil, not allow it to hurt us.

But power isn't his sole attribute.

God also is glorified by showing his wisdom. While his power gains our immediate praise, it often takes time for us to see his wisdom. One day in his presence, we'll marvel at his wisdom in *not* preventing certain evils that he used for our ultimate good.

Jerry Bridges wrote,

> If God is truly sovereign, if He truly loves you, and the teaching of Scripture is correct, then God will never allow any action against you that is not in accord with His ultimate purpose to work for your good. If the evil done against you is fresh and haunting, then I know my words may seem terribly calloused. But I say them because I believe they are true. Scripture teaches them, and one day we will all believe them, when we are with Him.[1]

One day. In the meantime, God calls every one of us to live by faith.

God's patience showcases his great mercy.

Paul asked, "What if God, choosing to show his wrath and make his power known, bore with great patience the objects of his wrath—prepared for destruction? What if he did this to make the riches of his glory known to the objects of his mercy, whom he prepared in advance for glory?" (Romans 9:22–23).

There's no room here to address the difficult issue of some people being described as "objects of [God's] wrath, prepared for destruction."

But that interpretive debate needn't distract us from the fact that God says he shows patience to those whom he ultimately will judge and shows mercy to his redeemed.

> God's glory is the highest good of the universe.

This passage parallels Ephesians 2:7, which adds that God's saving work in Christ, including his resurrection triumph, happened "in order that in *the coming ages* he might show the incomparable riches of his grace."

God's glory is the highest good of the universe. God knows that permitting evil and suffering—and paying the price to end them, as well as patiently delaying judgment and then bringing it decisively—will all ultimately reveal his character and cause his people to joyfully worship him forever.

God and Satan use the same pain with different objectives.

In 2 Corinthians 12:7 Paul said, "To keep me from becoming conceited because of these surpassingly great revelations, there was given me a thorn in my flesh." If the text stopped here, it would be obvious who gave the thorn in the flesh: God. Certainly the devil wouldn't want to prevent Paul from becoming conceited!

But Paul continued to describe the thorn in the flesh as "a messenger of Satan, to torment me." Two supernatural beings, adamantly opposed to each other, are said in a single verse to have distinct purposes in sending Paul a thorn in the flesh. God's purpose was not to torment him but to keep him from becoming conceited; Satan's purpose was to torment him and turn him from God.

In the next verses, Paul said he asked God three times to remove this "thorn," but God refused. The Lord did, however, reveal his purpose for not granting Paul's prayer request: "My grace is sufficient for you, for my power is made perfect in weakness" (verse 9).

Paul responded by rejoicing in his afflictions. Why? Because he knew God had a sovereign and loving purpose. We see this pattern repeatedly in the Bible:

- Joseph's brothers intended his sufferings for evil; God intended them for good.
- Satan intended Job's sufferings for evil; God intended them for good.
- Satan intended Jesus' sufferings for evil; God intended them for good.
- Satan intended Paul's sufferings for evil; God intended them for good.

So, if we're God's children, can't we add ourselves to this list?

- Satan intends *my* sufferings for evil; God intends them for good.
- Satan intends *your* sufferings for evil; God intends them for good.

With Joseph, Job, Jesus, and Paul—in all four cases, God's purpose prevailed. John wrote, "He who is in you is greater than he who is in the world" (1 John 4:4, ESV). Whose purpose are you furthering, Satan's or God's? Satan attempts to destroy your faith, while God invites you to draw upon his sovereign grace to sustain you.

If we recognize God's sovereignty and not Satan's, it changes our perspective. If God can use for good "a messenger of Satan," then surely he can use for good a car accident, our employer's unreasonable expectations, or even our own foolish mistakes.

You might not know whether your disease has been brought about by demons, human genetics under the Fall, a doctor's poor decision, or God's direct hand, but you know as much as you need to—that God is sovereign, and whether he heals your body now, ten years from now, or waits until the resurrection to do so, he desires to achieve his own good purpose in you.

Likewise, Satan sought Job's ruin and loss of faith; God sought Job's refining and faith building. The very thing Satan intended for Job's destruction, God intended for his betterment (though certainly at a terrible cost). Since this is Scripture, God intended it for our benefit as well (see 1 Corinthians 10:11). Satan and God intend the same suffering for entirely different purposes, but God's purpose triumphs—because he is sovereign and Satan is not.

God controls, but also permits and allows.

An ax head flies from its handle and kills someone. So what does God say? "If [the man] does not do it intentionally, but God lets it happen, he is to flee to a place I will designate" (Exodus 21:13). Moses didn't write that God caused the accident but rather he "lets it happen." The Contemporary English Version concurs with the ESV: "If you did not intend to kill someone, and I, the LORD, let it happen anyway..." The term "let" or "allow" or "permit" is also used by the NASB, RSV, CEB, NCV, NIRV, ESV, and NLT.

> If God can use for good "a messenger of Satan," then surely he can use for good even our own foolish mistakes.

We find similar language in Mark 5:12–13, where demons beg Jesus to send them into a herd of pigs and Jesus "gave them permission."

God said of disobedient people, "I let them become defiled...that I might fill them with horror so they would know that I am the LORD" (Ezekiel 20:26). God had a good purpose even in permitting terrible sin.

Sometimes God inhibits demonic and human choice. Jacob said of Laban, "God has not allowed him to harm me" (Genesis 31:7). God told Abimelech, "I have kept you from sinning against me" (Genesis 20:6). When casting out demons, Jesus "would not allow them to speak" (Luke 4:41).

I've heard people argue against saying "God allows" because they think "God causes" is more biblical and consistent with his sovereignty. But since Scripture uses the more passive "allow," "permit," or "let" along with the active "cause" and "make," why shouldn't we?

I deliberately focus here on God's permission rather than God's decrees, because it's common ground for different theological persuasions. But I want to make the rarely understood point that *divine permission is not passive and weak, but active and strong.* The more power someone has, the more significant his permission becomes. Me permitting my neighbor to cut down my tree blocking his view is one thing; the president permitting a general to move troops onto foreign soil is another.

God's "permitting" something is far stronger than it may at first appear. After all, whatever God permits actually happens. And as Joni Eareckson Tada put it, "God permits what he hates to achieve what he loves."[2]

The final chapter of the book of Job says his family and friends "comforted and consoled him over all the trouble the LORD had brought upon him" (42:11). So the inspired writer says God had brought Job's troubles on him. Yet early in the book God is said only to *permit* Satan to bring those troubles on Job (see 1:12). It appears here that the permission of God is more active than we often suppose. To allow evil with a definite purpose seems close to, if less direct than, the language of decreeing.

> The more power someone has, the more significant his permission becomes.

Although many find this truth disturbing, properly understood, it should comfort us. What should disturb us is the fallacy that God stands passively by while Satan, evildoers, diseases, and random accidents mar the lives of his beloved children. In fact, God allows (or sometimes brings) pain in our lives to help us become the people he desires us to be.

Real human choices cannot thwart God's sovereign plan.
In one sense, every murder, attack, and natural disaster confirms that God has permitted the world to violate his will, which C. S. Lewis called a sort of "divine abdication." But what if this apparent abdication is actually purposeful permission?

Scripture indicates that when an omnipotent God grants real and effectual choice, he doesn't lose power; he delegates it. That delegated power can be, and regularly is, abused. Yet God can and does still overrule and perform miracles of intervention.

Before sin, God gave people dominion over the world. In delegating this responsibility, God acted like a father who started a great business. Though he remains as owner and final decision maker, he has granted leadership powers to his children, who can do as they like (within certain limits). He chooses to subject his company to their decisions, good or bad.

Now suppose the manager of the universe can do what no human father could ever do: sovereignly use every decision, right or wrong, to accomplish an ultimate purpose. Could he not then be seen to maintain control even as he apparently abdicates it? This, I think, is what Scripture teaches.

Do we believe that in the instant a teenager's cell phone rings and he takes his eyes off the road, swerves, and kills a precious little girl on the sidewalk, all the good God planned for that girl and her family and friends dissolves into nothingness? Or do we believe God has a plan even in that dark moment and the moments that follow?

Corrie ten Boom, survivor of a Nazi concentration camp, loved to say that God is weaving a beautiful tapestry. While he sees from above its magnificence, we see only the knotted, tangled underside. But one day we'll see the tapestry's topside. Corrie never denied the evil or suffering she experienced, and neither should we. But God can weave the tapestry despite evil and suffering, using even the darkest threads in a finished work of startling beauty. One day we'll behold our own place in the design—and thank God profusely for putting us there.

Even "random" occurrences fit into God's sovereign design.

In a fascinating passage, evil King Ahab assembled his troops for war. Because a brave prophet told him, "The LORD has decreed disaster for you" (2 Chronicles 18:22), Ahab asked an allied king to go to battle in Ahab's royal attire, while Ahab dressed like a common soldier. That way, any enemy targeting King Ahab would miss him.

What happened? "But someone drew his bow at random and hit the king of Israel between the sections of his armor.... Then at sunset he died" (verses 33–34). Scripture uses the term "random" to describe the archer's action, but clearly God's hand directed that shaft. That "random" arrow had Ahab's name on it! While this passage doesn't prove God orchestrates every random occurrence, it does demonstrate that God has decreed that at least some "random" events accomplish eternal purposes.

> If the world is as random as some theologians suggest, then people, demons, and luck determine our destinies.

If God can use a "random" arrow, can't he have a purpose and plan in a tragic "accident" or an "unlucky" fall? Terrible events, heartbreaking as they are, do not lie beyond God's plan. The false notion of random events outside God's control sets us up for a lifetime of agonizing "what ifs" and "if onlys." *What if the doctor had looked at the x-rays more carefully two years ago?* Or, *What if the line had been shorter at the grocery store? Then I wouldn't have been at that intersection when the drunk driver ran the light, and my wife wouldn't have died.*

If the world is as random as some theologians suggest, it would seem that people, demons, and luck determine our destinies. We can drive ourselves crazy with such thoughts, or we can embrace God's sovereign purpose even in tragic events, thus affirming God's greatness.

God calls us not to victimization or to fatalism, but to faith in his character, promises, and purposes.

God allows only what he can use for the best.
Though I've referred to Romans 8:28 in several places, let's now take a closer look at it. This treasured (and often maligned) verse reads, "And we know that in all things God works for the good of those who love him, who have been called according to his purpose." That ultimate "good" includes the evil and suffering we endure.

If God cannot use something to contribute to the eternal good of his child, then he won't permit it to happen. I know of no other way to interpret this passage, written in a context of profound evil and suffering.

Different translations of Romans 8:28 suggest different nuances from the original Greek text. For those who love God, "all things work together for good" (ESV, KJV), "in all things God works for good" (GNT), "God causes all things to work together for good" (NASB).

In each case, the words "all things" are all inclusive. It doesn't say *some* or *most* things work together for our good, but *all* things. And what does "all things" *not* include? Three of these translations use the term "together," emphasizing a focus not on isolated events but on the sum of all events. It doesn't say "each thing *by itself is* good" but "all things work *together* for good" under God's sovereign hand.

Before my mother made a cake, she would lay all the ingredients on the kitchen counter. One day, I tasted each one. Baking powder. Baking soda. Eggs. Vanilla extract. I discovered that most cake ingredients taste terrible. But a remarkable metamorphosis took place when my mother mixed everything in the right amounts and baked them together. Based only on that earlier taste test of the ingredients, I never would have believed cake could be so delicious.

In a similar way, the individual ingredients of trials and tragedies taste bitter to us. Romans 8:28 doesn't tell me I should say "It is good" if I get robbed and beaten, or if my child dies. But when God carefully measures and mixes the ingredients, then raises the temperature, at just the right time he produces a perfect final product. God has mixed the not-so-tasty ingredients. He's baking the cake. We can smell it and get a first bite in this life. But the world where we'll sit down and eat that perfectly delicious cake is not this one, but the next.

God the Father wants us to become like Jesus.
We tend to define our good in terms of what brings us health and pleasure *now*. God defines it in terms of what makes us more like Jesus.

Paul's confidence that God is working "for good" implies ultimate good, not good feelings in suffering. As C. S. Lewis watched his wife, Joy, undergo cancer treatments, he wrote to a friend, "We are not necessarily doubting that God will do the best for us: we are wondering how painful the best will turn out to be."[3]

In Romans 8:29, Paul explained the basis on which he can claim that God works everything together for our good: "For those God foreknew he also predestined to be conformed to the likeness of his Son."

> Everything that comes into the life of God's child is Father-filtered.

Arminius said of foreknowledge in this verse, "God decreed to save and damn certain particular persons. This decree has its foundation in the foreknowledge of God, by which he knew from all eternity those individuals who *would,* through his prevenient grace, *believe,* and, through his subsequent grace *would persevere.*"[4]

Calvinists usually understand God's foreknowledge in this verse, not in terms of God knowing something about these people (such as whether or not they would believe in him), but that God knew the people themselves, marking them out and setting his heart upon them to enjoy a saving relationship with himself.

But both Calvinists and Arminians should agree this verse shows our highest calling as God's children: to be conformed to Christ. If God answered all our prayers to be delivered from evil and suffering, then he would be delivering us from Christlikeness.

Ten months after his son died, my friend, pastor Greg Laurie, told me, "What I wish is that I could have learned and grown and drawn close to the Lord *just like I have,* but that Christopher was still here." I too wish I could have the good God has brought me through adversity, without the loss. But as Greg and many of us know, it doesn't work that way.

Our doctrine of human free will must never lead us to believe our lives primarily depend on us or that God can't act unless we consent. Everything that comes into the life of God's child is Father-filtered. Whether suffering brings us to Christlikeness depends, to some degree, upon our choice to submit to and draw our strength from him. Suffering will come whether we allow it to make us more like Christ or not, but if we don't, we waste that suffering.

Spurgeon said, "Believing that God rules all, that he governs wisely, that he brings good out of evil, the believer's heart is assured, and he is enabled calmly to meet each trial as it comes."[5]

God displays his greatness by bringing good out of bad.

We judge a man's greatness by the size of the obstacles he overcomes. Climbing Mount Everest testifies to a climber's greatness precisely because of the mountain's enormity. An athlete who pole-vaults nine feet does nothing amazing, but one who pole-vaults twenty feet makes history.

So it is with the drama of redemption. Sin and death, Satan and his demons, the Hell we deserve—for God to demonstrate his greatness, he had to overcome all these powerful obstacles. The greater the obstacles, the greater the eternal glory to God.

Think about it: in a perfect, painless world, could we ever have come to know the surpassing majesty of God's sovereignty, wisdom, grace, mercy, patience, and love?

God's redemptive work also results in greater eternal praise of his sovereignty. We see something remarkable about a person who can bring some good out of bad. But what is most remarkable is to bring something incredibly good out of something desperately bad.

If the universe exists to demonstrate God's infinite greatness, then shouldn't we expect God to scale the highest redemptive mountain? The problems of death, evil, and suffering—and the extent of demonic and human rebellion—must be vast in order for God to show his superior greatness.

Every time we ask God to remove some obstacle, we should realize we may be asking him to forgo one more opportunity to declare his greatness. Certainly he sometimes graciously answers our prayers to relieve our suffering. This also testifies to his greatness, and we should praise him for answering yes. But when he answers no, we should recognize that he knows best.

Jerry Bridges helps us better understand this:

> Rather than being offended over the Bible's assertion of God's
> sovereignty in both good and calamity, believers should be
> comforted by it. Whatever our particular calamity or adversity
> may be, we may be sure that our Father has a loving purpose in
> it. As King Hezekiah said, "Surely it was for my benefit that I
> suffered such anguish" (Isaiah 38:17). God does not exercise His
> sovereignty capriciously, but only in such a way as His infinite
> love deems best for us.[6]

Our temporary suffering is not worthy of comparison with what God has planned for us.

Ten verses before Romans 8:28, Paul wrote something else that should
help us gain invaluable perspective: "I consider that our present sufferings are not worth comparing with the glory that will be revealed in us"
(verse 18).

Keep in mind that by the time Paul wrote the book of Romans, he'd
endured far more suffering than most of us ever will: beatings, imprison-
ments, hunger, slander, utter destitution, shipwrecks, stoning, and more
(see 2 Corinthians 11:23–29). He learned his theology in the rough and
tumble of life, not in a comfy armchair before a warm fire.

> The Bible encourages us to use our
> memories of God's past acts of providence
> to increase our trust in his present and
> future providence.

Paul had already traveled such a hard road that he could write, "If
only for this life we have hope in Christ, we are to be pitied more than all
men" (1 Corinthians 15:19). Paul had chosen a life of such severe hardships that if he had nothing to anticipate other than the pleasures of this

world, he would consider himself no more than a pitiable fool. Therefore he also wrote, "If I fought wild beasts in Ephesus for merely human reasons, what have I gained?" If there's no eternal resurrected life, Paul judged that everyone would be better off endorsing the Epicurean philosophy of "Let us eat and drink, for tomorrow we die" (verse 32).

But Paul didn't endorse such a philosophy. Instead he fully anticipated and expected to be raised with Christ into an eternity so packed with wonders that he had no words to describe its glory. That's why he could truthfully say that our present sufferings aren't worth comparing with the glory we'll experience.

When we acknowledge the suffering and pain of this life—but look forward to a glorious future with God in which the worst hardships here can't compare to the least joys there—we find strength and encouragement to finish our course. While no current explanation (including mine) of our suffering on earth can suffice, Paul assures us that our eventual experience in eternity will more than suffice.

Will we believe him? That's a choice each of us—regardless of our theological persuasions—must make.

Notes

The second epigraph is from Anonymous, quoted in Jerry Bridges, *Is God Really in Control? Trusting God in a World of Hurt* (Colorado Springs, CO: NavPress, 2006), 19.

1. Bridges, *Is God Really in Control?*, 50.

2. Joni Eareckson Tada and Steven Estes, *When God Weeps* (Grand Rapids, MI: Zondervan, 1997), 84.

3. C. S. Lewis, *Letters of C. S. Lewis,* ed. W. H. Lewis (Boston: Mariner Books, 2003), 477.

4. Jacobus Arminius, *The Works of James Arminius, D.D.,* trans. James Nichols (Auburn, NY: Derby, Miller and Orton, 1853), 1:248.

5. C. H. Spurgeon, *Morning and Evening: Daily Readings,* August 5, morning, www.ccel.org/ccel/spurgeon/morneve.d0805am.html.

6. Bridges, *Is God Really in Control?*, 20.

Concluding Thoughts on Sovereignty, Choice, Calvinism, and Arminianism

O Sovereign LORD, you have only begun to show
your greatness and the strength of your hand to me,
your servant. Is there any god in heaven or on earth
who can perform such great and mighty deeds as
you do?

Deuteronomy 3:24, NLT

A God less than sovereign could not bestow moral
freedom upon His creatures. He would be afraid to
do so.

A. W. Tozer

Early in the book I raised the issue of Calvinists and Arminians misrepresenting each other's positions. It's also true that we tend, understandably, to become deeply entrenched in our own positions.

Those who grew up in church may not realize how deeply vested they are in the theology in which they and their families were immersed. For the first ten years of my Christian life I saw faith through an Arminian lens. But I hadn't grown up in a Christian home, so it was easier for me to gradually depart from some of my early Christian beliefs because they hadn't been as long woven into my core identity.

It's sometimes hard for those who've always been Calvinists to realize their own vested interests in all things Calvinism. Many have never known a different way of thinking and have long believed Arminianism to be a false gospel. (The fact is, there are both Calvinists and Arminians who preach a true gospel and false ones—you can't know until you hear what they really believe.)

As a mostly Calvinist who was once mostly Arminian, I understand the arguments for and against both positions. I've become comfortable in my Reformed beliefs, but I've noticed I'm not as quick to draw lines in the sand as some of my Calvinist friends. Some seem ready to assume the worst, pouncing when someone phrases a sentence in a way they aren't accustomed to—one that "sounds Arminian." Often, I find that when I ask people what they mean, there is no underlying heresy. Of course, sometimes there is, but when I've asked with humility (not pouncing), I have a much better opportunity to offer, as well as receive, gentle correction from Scripture.

Some Arminians may object to my having departed their fold. Since I describe myself as 80 percent Calvinist, some Calvinists will be frustrated that I haven't bought into "the whole package." To them, Calvinism is a seamless garment, all or nothing. They suppose I'm uninformed and in need of a long e-mail, or that I'm really—God help me—an Arminian in disguise! (Trust me, I've had those conversations.)

There was a time years ago when I avoided telling Arminian friends that I was crossing over to Calvinism, which was roughly equivalent to the "dark side."

I also found that as I became more Calvinistic, my instinct was to want to join the club and carry the card. Yet I couldn't read certain passages without concluding that Christ died for all sinners. So I landed at four-point Calvinism, a position popular with no one but four-point Calvinists.

Many of us, when we study the Bible, will never enter into any theological system 100 percent. And that shouldn't be our goal, should it? Let's seek consistency with Scripture, not with Calvinism or Arminianism. If we're not careful, our logic, or the logic of brilliant theologians we respect, can become our real authority. But that position should be reserved for God's Word alone.

I no longer care whether I completely fit in. I'm happy seeking to be true to God's Word, just like many Arminians and five-point Calvinists who've come to some different conclusions than I have.

Calvinists often act just like Arminians, and Arminians like Calvinists.

When I was an Arminian, the Bible's sovereignty texts were a great comfort to me; I celebrated God's grace in delivering me from the darkness of sin and welcoming me into his family. As a Calvinist, I have a deep concern to get the gospel to people, to see God's Word translated into the languages of all the world's people groups, and to fight hunger, sex trafficking, and the killing of unborn children.

I find that even Calvinists who argue against "free will" live and talk and preach as if they have it, and everyone else does too, including unbelievers. They commend those who choose well and criticize those who choose poorly. They wouldn't do this unless they believed those were real choices made by those who might have chosen to the contrary.

I find that Arminians who say they believe God always respects the free will of people, never imposing his will on them, often passionately pray that God would intervene to change the hearts of friends and loved ones and to bring them to faith in Jesus.

For instance, evangelist Jerry Falwell, a good brother, once said to an audience, "He will not force you against your will to come to the cross." Then he closed in prayer and said to God, "Do not let one person say 'no' to your precious will. Save the lost." Think about it—how can God not let people say no if he never constrains them to say yes?

In real life, Calvinists rarely if ever take strict determinism to its logical conclusions, and Arminians rarely if ever take strict libertarianism to its logical conclusions. In my opinion this is a good thing. What we should take most seriously in forming our habits of thinking, action, prayer, and evangelism is not our theological systems but Scripture.

Read the books Calvinists and Arminians write—not just what their opponents say they believe.

It's easy to set up straw men that we can easily tear down. I was once sent an audio recording in which a seminary professor speaking to pastors systematically tore apart a particular theological position that happened to be mine. He misrepresented that position, and the pastors listening laughed aloud at how ridiculous it was. While I shook my head at his unfair characterization, it dawned on me how often, without knowing it, I'd probably misrepresented *his* position.

In my experience, Arminians don't read enough written by Calvinists, nor do Calvinists read enough written by Arminians. The result of this can be not only misunderstanding but also presumption, arrogance, and a judgmental attitude. Some Calvinists say to Arminians, "You don't believe in God's sovereignty"; some Arminians say to Calvinists, "You don't believe in God's love." Both *do* believe in God's sovereignty and love, but they see God as working out those attributes differently.

We can certainly disagree, even vigorously. But we need to be careful not to slander brothers and sisters who love Jesus and believe his Word. Jesus said, "I tell you, on the day of judgment people will give account for every careless word they speak" (Matthew 12:36, ESV). We won't be granted a pass by saying, "But, Lord, I won that argument."

There's a shocking amount of secondhand "knowledge" among Christians that's just plain wrong. John Wesley asked an excellent question in this regard: "How can any man know what Arminius held, who has never read one page of his writings? Let no man bawl against Arminians, till he knows what the term means; and then he will know that Arminians and Calvinists are just upon a level."[1]

While I find much more to disagree with in reading Arminius than I do Calvin, I often agree with Arminius and sometimes disagree with Calvin.

A Calvinist pastor at a Reformed church was challenged by a friend to read the works of Arminius. He'd been taught that Arminius was So-cinian (denying the Trinity as well as the deity of Christ) and Pelagian (believing in salvation by works). After reading Arminius he wrote, "I was surprised how Calvinist his affirmations sounded about trinitarian-ism, Scripture, original sin and the necessity of grace."[2]

I too have been amazed at some of the actual writings of Arminius, much of which any Calvinist would concur with—as long as he didn't know it was written by Arminius!

Arminius said,

> Free will is unable to begin or to perfect any true and spiritual
> good, without grace.... I mean by it that which is the grace of
> Christ and which belongs to regeneration. I affirm, therefore, that
> this grace is simply and absolutely necessary for the illumination
> of the mind, the due ordering of the affections, and the inclina-
> tion of the will to that which is good.... This grace goes before,
> accompanies, and follows; it excites, assists, operates that we will,
> and co-operates lest we will in vain.[3]

What about the work of God and the condition of the human heart? Arminius wrote, "This grace commences salvation, promotes it, and per-fects and consummates it. I confess that the mind of a natural and carnal man is obscure and dark, that his affections are corrupt and inordinate, that his will is stubborn and disobedient, and that the man himself is dead in sins."[4]

Arminius, like Calvin, was a Reformer. That doesn't mean he was always right, of course. But he was right about far more things than most Calvinists would suspect if they've never read him. And how many Ar-minians read Calvin? Most people aren't tempted to read the writings of someone they've been told was a bloodthirsty tyrant who believed in a monstrous God. Yet when I read Calvin, that's certainly not the impres-sion I get.

It's easy to be clever and biblically keen when refuting a position no one actually believes. It requires little skill, grace, or intelligence. What's much harder is to listen to someone's best arguments and, knowing what they really believe, engage in civil, intelligent debate. That's why it's important to let Arminians, the Reformed, dispensationalists, charismatics, cessationists, and others actually speak for themselves, rather than listen to other people's dismissive summaries of their positions. Any position appears preposterous when stated by its critics, but it will often sound sensible, even persuasive, when stated by its advocates.

Calvinists, I encourage you to read *What the Bible Says About God the Ruler*[5] by Jack Cottrell, an Arminian book on God's sovereignty. Sure, I disagree with Cottrell in important areas. But he is biblically informed, logical, articulate, and respectful of God's Word.

Arminians, read *Trusting God*[6] by Jerry Bridges, on God's sovereignty. You'll disagree with some points, but you'll also find your mind enlightened and your heart moved. Michael Horton's *For Calvinism* and Roger Olson's *Against Calvinism* are also good resources; compare their arguments with Scripture and each other.[7]

If you have learned something on your own from *hand in Hand*, consider reading and discussing it in a group, respectfully listening and growing together.

I like people who can see how their theological viewpoints are sometimes poorly represented by their advocates. Resolute Calvinist Douglas Wilson says, "Calvinism without Jesus is deadly; it's fatalism, it's simply Islam. We need Jesus. When the precious doctrines [of Calvinism] are used to perpetuate gloom, severity, introspection, accusations, morbidity, slander, gnat-stringing, and more, the soul is not safe."[8]

When you read Scripture, always ask, "What does this text of Scripture not say that I might have expected it to?"
When I read Scripture I try to notice not only what the text says but also what it doesn't say. Take this statement of Jesus: "No one can come to me unless the Father who sent me draws him" (John 6:44, ESV). Arminians, why didn't he say, "No one can come to me unless he so chooses"? Or "Anyone can come to me, since he's free either to choose me or not"?

Or take this word from Paul: "[God] desires all people to be saved and to come to the knowledge of the truth" (1 Timothy 2:4, ESV). Calvinists, why didn't Paul say, "God has chosen, and so desires, only his elect to be saved and to come to the knowledge of the truth"?

Jesus said, "Many are invited, but few are chosen" (Matthew 22:14, GNT). Arminians, why didn't he say, "Many are invited but few choose to come"? Calvinists, why didn't he say, "God only invites those he has chosen"?

Acts 27 is a passage dealing with physical deliverance, not spiritual salvation, but it serves as an interesting illustration of God's sovereignty and human choice. In a ship at sea overtaken by a relentless storm, Paul pronounced unconditionally to his shipmates, "I urge you to take heart, for there will be no loss of life among you, but only of the ship" (verse 22, ESV). He told them an angel had revealed this to him, saying, "God has granted you all those who sail with you" (verse 24, ESV). There it is. The matter was settled by the decree of God.

Later their situation only worsened, so that "the sailors were seeking to escape from the ship, and had lowered the ship's boat into the sea" (verse 30, ESV). Paul then told the soldiers on board, "Unless these men stay in the ship, you cannot be saved" (verse 31, ESV). As a result, "the soldiers cut away the ropes of the ship's boat and let it go" (verse 32, ESV).

But wait. God had decreed that all these men would be saved. How could Paul now say that unless everyone stayed on the ship, the remaining men could *not* be saved? Why did Paul encourage the soldiers to take human action as if the outcome depended on them, rather than on the stated decree of God?

These two tenets that appear contradictory to us were simultaneously embraced by Paul with no apparent difficulty. One appears decidedly Calvinistic, the other decidedly Arminian. Do you see the beauty in that? Of course, some Calvinists will argue nothing in the passage is Arminian, and Arminians can do exactly the reverse. But this is because we're accustomed to explaining away and reinterpreting those "other Scriptures" to fit our systems. As a result we often fail to see *all* that the

Bible actually says. Too often, we walk away from Scripture not having learned all that God desires to teach us.

All positions have strengths and weaknesses; be sure you know the strengths of others and the weaknesses of your own.
Let's not hold those who disagree with us to standards of biblical evidence that we don't require of our own beliefs. Jesus said, "Treat others the same way you want them to treat you" (Luke 6:31, NASB).

If you think of your position on sovereignty and meaningful choice as the one without problems, you're not seeing accurately. All the positions have snags.

> If I come to God's Word unguarded, shields down, God uses it to grab me, taking me where he wants me to go.

When I was an Arminian, I never believed I was to be congratulated for my merit in choosing Christ. I believed the Scripture that said God had drawn me to him and knew that he deserved all praise for my conversion. I believed God was sovereign, though I didn't believe he was as involved in the small details of my life as I now do, nor that I could be certain in this life that he had a plan in all that happened to me.

As a Calvinist, I don't for a moment believe people are robots or that God doesn't care about most of the human race. I believe he loved the world so much that he went to the cross to purchase redemption, and that he makes to all people a meaningful offer of salvation in Christ—salvation that he gets the credit for, but which we are fully responsible for if we reject it. The gospel is for the whole world.

Classical Arminianism is orthodox, but if you don't stick with God's Word, beware: it could set you on a trajectory toward the heresies of open theism or semi-Pelagianism. Mainstream Calvinism is orthodox, but beware: it could set you on a trajectory toward the heresies of hyper-Calvinism or fatalism.

The bottom line is this: be willing to have "leaks" and inconsistencies in your theological system, but be unwilling to reject portions of Scripture.

When I read books arguing against my position, they often cite passages I tend to ignore. I try to reflect on those passages. I try to allow God's Word to surprise me and change my mind and modify my positions. I like to learn. If I come to God's Word unguarded, with my shields down, God uses it to grab me, taking me where *he* wants me to go. If the Bible never changes your mind because you've already got everything figured out, you're missing the joy of discovery.

Scripture should be continually renewing our minds (see Romans 12:1–2). Do you have a Bible in which you underline, as I do? Sometimes I take a careful look at the passages of Scripture I *haven't* underlined. Then I ask God to teach me from the inspired words I've overlooked.

The sovereign God of grace, who grants meaningful choice to his creatures, is worthy of our heartfelt praise.
Truth is important. It sets us free (see John 8:32). When we love God and others, we can speak the truth in love (see Ephesians 4:15). We can respectfully engage others in discussions about the relationship between God's sovereignty and human choice, and other issues too. Putting Scripture on the table, we might even persuade others of truth, or be persuaded by them.

Though we're incapable of solving the deep mysteries of God, we're fully capable of learning and appreciating more about them: "Oh, the depth of the riches and wisdom and knowledge of God! How unsearchable are his judgments and how inscrutable his ways!" (Romans 11:33, esv).

The Good News Translation renders Acts 17:11, "The people there were more open-minded than the people in Thessalonica. They listened to the message with great eagerness, and every day they studied the Scriptures to see if what Paul said was really true."

May we be like those people: open-minded, eager students of the very words of God.

Regardless of our different understandings of the interworking of sovereignty and meaningful choice, all who love Jesus and are saved by his sovereign grace alone can walk hand in Hand with our God and with each other, united in praise for him.

Let me end with a Puritan prayer from *The Valley of Vision:*

SOVEREIGN GOD,
Thy cause, not my own, engages my heart,
and I appeal to thee with greatest freedom
to set up thy kingdom in every place where Satan reigns;
Glorify thyself and I shall rejoice,
for to bring honor to thy name is my sole desire.
I adore thee that thou art God,
and long that others should know it, feel it, and rejoice in it.
O that all men might love and praise thee,
that thou mightest have all glory.[9]

Notes

The second epigraph is from A. W. Tozer, *The Knowledge of the Holy* (San Francisco, CA: HarperOne, 1992), 122.

1. John Wesley, *The Works of the Reverend John Wesley, A. M.,* ed. John Emory (New York: J. Collord, 1831), 6:134.

2. Mark A. Ellis, in the introduction to *The Arminian Confession of 1621,* trans. and ed. Mark A. Ellis (Eugene, OR: Pickwick Publications, 2005), v.

3. Jacobus Arminius, *The Works of James Arminius, D.D.,* trans. James Nichols (Auburn, NY: Derby, Miller and Orton, 1853), 2:472.

4. Arminius, *Works,* 2:473.

5. Jack Cottrell, *What the Bible Says About God the Ruler* (Eugene, OR: Wipf and Stock, 2000).

6. Jerry Bridges, *Trusting God: Even When Life Hurts* (Carol Stream, IL: NavPress, 2008).

7. Michael S. Horton, *For Calvinism* (Grand Rapids, MI: Zondervan, 2011) and Roger E. Olson, *The Story of Christian Theology: Twenty Centuries of Tradition and Reform* (Downers Grove, IL: InterVarsity, 1999).

8. Douglas Wilson, "Undragoned: C.S. Lewis on the Gift of Salvation" (speech, plenary session, Desiring God National Conference, September 2013), www.desiringgod.org/blog/posts/15-quotes-from-the-c-s-lewis-conference.

9. Arthur Bennett, *The Valley of Vision: A Collection of Puritan Prayers and Devotions* (Edinburgh: Banner of Truth Trust, 2003), 177.

Small-Group
Discussion Questions

Use the following questions to stimulate your personal reflection as well as for group discussion. You can also access these questions online and print them with space for answers: www.epm.org/handinhand/questions.

Chapter 1: Why Is This Tough and Controversial Issue Worth Discussing?

1. Respond to this statement: The issue of God's sovereignty and human freedom isn't important. Doctrine doesn't matter; it's all about following Jesus.
2. On page 2, the author affirms our need "to *better* understand what we cannot *fully* understand." Do you find the idea of studying a subject we can't wrap our minds around frustrating or intriguing? Why?
3. In your family or church background, was greater emphasis put on sovereignty or free will? How has that affected your own thinking?
4. What questions do you have about the relationship of God's sovereignty and free will?
5. One of the stated purposes of this book (page 5) is "to prevent us from becoming trivial people in a shallow age." Do you think this is a serious danger?
6. Do you agree that "everything about God, including his choices, is greater than everything about us" (page 7)? How does your answer affect your thinking concerning this subject?
7. Choose at least one Scripture and one statement in this chapter that you find particularly significant. Why are they significant to you?

Chapter 2: An Invitation to Calvinists, Arminians, and Those Who Don't Know the Difference

1. Before reading this chapter, how familiar were you with the terms "Calvinist" and "Arminian"?
2. How would you explain the similarities and differences between Calvinism and Arminianism?
3. While recognizing real differences between Calvinism and Arminianism, the author says, "Let's not condemn people for what we've heard they believe. Let's ask them what they really do believe."
   a. Have you had experience discussing Calvinism and Arminianism? Was it good or bad or some of both?
   b. Have your beliefs ever been misconstrued by unbelievers or fellow believers? How did that feel?
   c. How can we avoid misrepresenting those we disagree with while respectfully maintaining our disagreement when needed?
4. a. On page 27 the author lays out a partial list of orthodox doctrines. Are there any you would add or remove?
   b. Do you agree that some Calvinists and some Arminians are orthodox; that is, they hold to the essential doctrines of the Christian faith?
5. In examining the five-point tables on pages 18–20 and the ten different doctrinal issues on pages 23–25, do you find yourself more on the Calvinist or Arminian side? Are there some exceptions?
6. A. W. Tozer said, "Nothing less than a whole Bible can make a whole Christian." What are the consequences of embracing selected parts of Scripture?
7. Choose at least one Scripture and one statement in this chapter that you find particularly significant. Why are they significant to you?

Chapter 3: The Sovereignty of God

1. How does a Calvinist's and an Arminian's view of God's sovereignty differ?
2. What Scripture passages mentioned do you find troubling or difficult to understand?
3. How does God's sovereignty relate to the evil and suffering we see in this world? (Share relevant Scripture.)
4. The author quotes his friend with cerebral palsy as saying, "God tailors a package of suffering best suited for each of his own" (page 46). Do you see that statement supported in Scripture? Does this comfort or encourage you?
5. The author states, "We can trust God's loving sovereignty in every hardship." Give examples of how you have experienced that trust or seen it in others' lives.
6. What biblical characters come to mind in whose lives God used suffering for their good and his glory?
7. How should we respond when God allows or brings suffering into our lives?
8. Choose at least one Scripture and one statement in this chapter that you find particularly significant. Why are they significant to you?

Chapter 4: Free Will and Meaningful Choice

1. a. How would you define "free will"?
   b. In what ways are human beings free, and in what ways are we not free or is our freedom limited?
2. The author likes the term "meaningful choice." Can a choice that is only partly free still be meaningful and consequential?
3. The author says that "contrary choice" can be either a biblical or unbiblical notion, depending on how we define it (pages 59–61). How would you explain contrary choice?

4. What is "prevenient" grace? Why is it a particularly important Arminian belief to understand?

5. The author talks about the terms "total depravity" and "total inability" (pages 67–69). How do these relate to human choice?

6. a. How could the belief *that no matter what decisions we make, God has predetermined our every thought and action,* affect us negatively?

   b. How could seeing ourselves as "masters of our fate" affect us negatively?

7. Are believers freer or less free than unbelievers? How are our new natures, sanctification, and the Holy Spirit involved in this?

8. Though freedom of choice complicates our lives and opens the door to suffering, why should we be grateful for it?

9. Choose at least one Scripture and one statement in this chapter that you find particularly significant. Why are they significant to you?

Chapter 5: Main Views of Sovereignty and Choice

1. What are the differences between the *libertarian, determinist,* and *compatibilist* views?

2. Which of those terms would you apply to your own beliefs? Have you always held your current view?

3. What verses in this chapter do you find yourself most in danger of neglecting?

4. How did Spurgeon's views about election and God's sovereignty affect his sharing of the gospel?

5. a. How would you explain "The Wills of God" chart on page 102?

   b. Does saying "God is sovereignly accomplishing his will" mean that God approves of everything that happens?
   Why is it important to clarify the term "God's will"?

6. How did this chapter challenge or reinforce your view of God's sovereignty and human choices?

7. What did you learn about the other side of the argument in this chapter (whichever side you disagree with)?

8. Choose at least one Scripture and one statement in this chapter that you find particularly significant. Why are they significant to you?

Chapter 6: Does Open Theism Resolve the Sovereignty/Choice Paradox?

1. How would you define "open theism"?

2. Does the Bible teach God's full knowledge of all things—past, present, and future? Support your answer from Scripture.

3. Have you ever found yourself wanting to redefine God or reduce him to a single attribute (for example, love or holiness)? Why is that dangerous?

4. Does open theism's view of God attract or concern you? Why?

5. Do you agree that open theism goes beyond the bounds of biblical and orthodox Christianity? Why or why not?

6. Do you find comfort in God's exhaustive knowledge of the future? Why or why not?

7. Choose at least one Scripture and one statement in this chapter that you find particularly significant. Why are they significant to you?

Chapter 7: The Fascinating Interplay of God's Sovereignty and Human Choice

1. Which diagrams in this chapter come closest to depicting your views?

2. The author notes that Scripture seldom struggles with the relationship between God's sovereignty and our choices. Why do you think many of us struggle with this issue?

3. How does the author's statement "Meaningful choice is essential for genuine love" (page 144) deepen your understanding of God's love *and* our love toward him and each other?

4. How might our freedom be the same and different after we are with Christ?

5. Since God *can* overrule our choices, why doesn't he do so to keep us from hurting ourselves and others?

6. Choose at least one Scripture and one statement in this chapter that you find particularly significant. Why are they significant to you?

Chapter 8: Meaningful Human Choice and Divine Sovereignty Working hand in Hand

1. Does the imagery of our small hand being in God's big Hand appeal to you? Why or why not?

2. How would you state a version of the "passengers on the ocean-going ship" analogy (pages 152–53) that expresses your understanding of sovereignty and meaningful choice?

3. Do you agree that we sometimes force Scripture into a box that fits our background and preferences, rather than letting it speak for itself? Why do you suppose we do this?

4. Reread the two numbered lists on pages 158–59 from D. A. Carson—one with four points on God's sovereignty, the next with nine on human choices. Which ones are hardest for you to believe?

5. The author states, "Scripture often portrays God's choices and human choices as intertwined" (page 162). Looking at the related diagrams, how would you explain this coexistence?

6. a. Do you agree that the biblical worldview is not fatalistic?

   b. What is our calling from God toward the broken world around us?

7. a. Can "trusting God" become an excuse for being lazy? How?

   b. Have you found a balance between doing your part while depending on God to do his?

8. Is the offer of the gospel universal or just for some? Support your answer biblically.

9. Choose at least one Scripture and one statement in this chapter that you find particularly significant. Why are they significant to you?

Chapter 9: Voices from the Past Share Timeless Truths

1. What did C. S. Lewis mean when he spoke of "chronological snobbery" (page 178)? Do you agree this is a problem for modern believers?
2. The author, with support from Spurgeon (pages 180–81), affirms the importance of sound doctrine but says, "While the Bible is God breathed, theological systems are not." Have you ever granted too much authority to a system or a person at the expense of biblical authority?
3. The author tells the story of Charles Simeon, the Calvinist, speaking with John Wesley, the Arminian (pages 182–85). Do you find this story helpful?
4. The author quotes Arminius as enthusiastically recommending the commentaries of John Calvin (page 188). What does this tell you about Arminius? About Calvin?
5. Proverbs 6:16, 19 says God hates "a man who stirs up dissension among brothers."
   a. Do you think this passage sometimes applies to people fixated on a theological viewpoint? When?
   b. What motivation do you find in this chapter for being gracious toward those with whom you have theological differences?
6. Choose at least one Scripture and one statement in this chapter that you find particularly significant. Why are they significant to you?

Chapter 10: Trusting God to Weave All Choices Together for His Children's Good

1. a. What is God's perspective on our suffering? Does he have purpose in it?
   b. How can suffering make us more like Jesus?
2. What promises from the Bible can you cling to in difficult times?

3. Have you seen God bring good out of something terrible that happened to you?

4. Genesis 50:20 implies that Satan intends your sufferings for evil while God intends them for good. Do you agree? How does that affect your perspective?

5. From God's perspective, is any circumstance random or any outcome uncertain? Support your answer scripturally.

6. Choose at least one Scripture and one statement in this chapter that you find particularly significant. Why are they significant to you?

Chapter 11: Concluding Thoughts on Sovereignty, Choice, Calvinism, and Arminianism

1. The author observes how we tend "to become deeply entrenched in our own positions" (page 209). How have you seen this to be true in your life?

2. The author discusses further engaging with this issue by reading books of a different persuasion or with multiple authors presenting their own positions. Which books would you like to read next?

3. How has reading *hand in Hand* helped you...
   a. in relationship to God's sovereignty and our choices?
   b. in your approach to Scripture?
   c. in your view of the value of doctrine?
   d. in your understanding and graciousness toward people with different positions?

4. Has this study impacted your relationship with God? How?

5. How would you explain to someone both the strengths and weaknesses of your position on God's sovereignty and human choice?

6. Choose at least one Scripture and one statement in this chapter that you find particularly significant. Why are they significant to you?

About the Author

Randy Alcorn is an author and the founder and director of Eternal Perspective Ministries (EPM), a nonprofit ministry dedicated to teaching principles of God's Word and assisting the church in ministering to the unreached, unfed, unborn, uneducated, unreconciled, and unsupported people around the world. His ministry focus is communicating the strategic importance of using our earthly time, money, possessions, and opportunities to invest in need-meeting ministries that count for eternity. He accomplishes this by analyzing, teaching, and applying biblical truth.

Before starting EPM in 1990, Randy served as a pastor for fourteen years. He has an MA degree in Biblical Studies from Multnomah University and an honorary doctorate from Western Seminary in Portland, Oregon, and has taught on the adjunct faculties of both.

A *New York Times* best-selling author, Randy has written more than forty books including *Heaven*, *The Treasure Principle*, *If God Is Good*, and the award-winning novel *Safely Home*. His books have sold over eight million copies and have been translated into over fifty languages. Randy has written for many magazines including EPM's issues-oriented magazine *Eternal Perspectives*. He is active daily on Facebook and Twitter, and has been a guest on more than seven hundred radio, television, and online programs including *Focus on the Family*, *FamilyLife Today*, *Revive Our Hearts*, *The Bible Answer Man*, and *The Resurgence*.

Randy resides in Gresham, Oregon, with his wife, Nanci. They have two married daughters and are the proud grandparents of five grandsons. Randy enjoys hanging out with his family, biking, tennis, underwater photography, research, and reading.

You may contact Eternal Perspective Ministries at www.epm.org, info@epm.org, or 39085 Pioneer Blvd., Suite 206, Sandy, OR 97055 or 503-668-5200.

Follow Randy on

Facebook: www.facebook.com/randyalcorn

Twitter: www.twitter.com/randyalcorn

Blog: www.epm.org/blog

FLIP-FLOP YOUR CONCEPT OF GIVING!

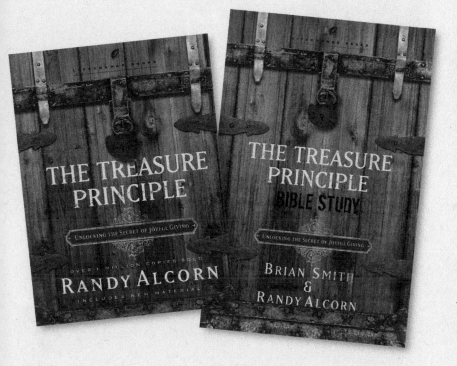

When Jesus told His followers to "lay up for yourselves treasures in heaven," He intended that they discover an astounding secret: how joyful giving brings God maximum glory and His children maximum pleasure. Discover a joy more precious than gold!

If You've Ever Asked Yourself If God Is Good...

Explore the goodness of God to uncover the hopeful truth.

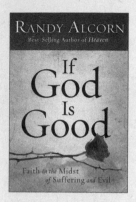

A comprehensive examination of God's goodness in the context of suffering and evil.

A special introductory booklet, available as a 10-pack. Ideal for distribution to grief support group members or as a gift for a loved one struggling with loss.

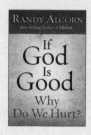

Companion to core book. Includes an option for 4-week, 8-week, and 13-week study, for groups and individuals.

A specially focused condensation that explores the personal issues of faith as it relates to suffering and evil.

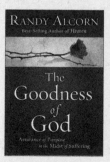

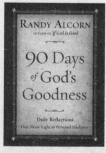

Daily devotional reflections that shine light on personal darkness.